Courtesy of the Steamship Historical Society of America.

THE GRAND DAME OF THE SEA

"She seems almost alive."
—Peter Gimbel

Postcard of the *Andrea Doria*.

Andrea Doria advertisement.

ANDREA DORIA

DIVE TO AN ERA

BY

GARY GENTILE

GARY GENTILE PRODUCTIONS
P.O. Box 57137
Philadelphia, PA 19111
1989

Gary Gentile Productions
P.O. Box 57137
Philadelphia, PA 19111

Additional copies may be purchased for $25 U.S. each, postage paid. Checks and money orders accepted.

Picture Credits

Unless otherwise specified, all photographs were taken by the author. The dust jacket front cover shows Tom Packer and the *Andrea Doria's* bell moments after it was discovered. The dust jacket rear cover shows the *Andrea Doria* in her home port (Courtesy Italian Line). The dust jacket rear inside flap shows the author with the *Andrea Doria's* bell the day after its recovery. All pictures of Peter Gimbel are courtesy of Elga Andersen.

The author wishes to acknowledge Hank Keatts for his valuable advice; Dave Bright and Bill Campbell for sharing the efforts of their research; Steve Gatto and Jon Hulburt for the use of their photographs; Glenn Garvin and Dan and Joni Turner for their hospitality; and Elga Andersen for encouragement, assistance, friendship, and strict adherence to detail.

International Standard Book Number (ISBN) 0-9621453-0-0

First Edition

Printed in Hong Kong

ANDREA DORIA
Dive to an Era

by
Gary Gentile

IN MEMORIUM

Peter Gimbel

February 14, 1928 – July 12, 1987

Statistics

Andrea Doria

29,083 gross tons (displacement)
700.0 feet overall length (656.5 feet at the waterline)
90.2 feet breadth
45.4 feet depth
Built by Ansaldo Shipyards, at Sestri, near Genoa, Italy
Owned by "Italia" Societa per Azioni di Navigatione (Italian Line)
Port of Registry: Genoa, Italy
Accommodations: 1,241 passengers—218 first class
320 cabin class
703 tourist class
Crew: 575
Power: 6 steam turbines fitted for oil fuel, turning twin screws
Cruising speed: 23 knots (26.45 statute miles per hour)

Stockholm

11,650 gross tons (displacement)
524.7 feet overall length (510.4 feet at the waterline)
69.1 feet breadth
32.7 feet depth
Built by A/B Gotaverken, at Gothenburg, Sweden (1948)
Owned by A/B Svenska Amerika Linien (Swedish American Line)
Port of Registry: Gothenburg, Sweden
Accommodations: 548 passengers
Power: 2 diesel engines turning twin screws

Timetable of Major Events

1950 February—*Andrea Doria's* keel laid
1951 June—*Andrea Doria* launched
1953 January—Maiden voyage of the *Andrea Doria*
1956 July 25 (11:10 p.m)—*Andrea Doria* collides with the *Stockholm*
1956 July 26 (10:09 a.m.)—*Andrea Doria* sinks
1956 July 27—Gimbel and Fox are first divers on the wreck
1956 August—Gimbel and MacLeish (*Life*)
1956 September—Dumas and Malle
1957 August—Gimbel
1964 July and August—*Top Cat* (Garvin and Solomon)
1966 August—Gimbel
1968 July—Vailati
1968 October—Krasberg and Zinkowski
1973 July 24 to August 17—Saturation Systems (Rodocker and DeLucchi)
1975 August—Gimbel
1981 July 29 to September 1—Gimbel

Courtesy of the U.S. Coast Guard.

FOREWORD

"Where there is an open mind there will always be a frontier."
—Charles Kettering

Courtesy of the U.S. Coast Guard.

Courtesy of the U.S. Coast Guard.

Foreword

People asked to name some famous shipwrecks invariably rattle off the big three: the *Titanic*, the *Lusitania*, and the *Andrea Doria*. Yet the most renowned wreck of all, one with which everyone has been familiar since childhood, seldom comes to mind.

The venerable Captain Noah performed spectacular feats of seamanship unequalled in modern times. Although he built his ship in the middle of a forest, far from the sea, he was wise enough to employ a subcontractor to handle the launching. Once on the bounding main he survived the most ferocious storm in the history of mankind, rivaling those dreaded North Atlantic tempests and South Pacific typhoons.

Driven by an almighty wind that buffeted his frail craft for nearly seven weeks, Noah reefed his sails and maintained a constant vigil at the helm. He ignored the unceasing rain, and fought off monstrous waves the likes of which have never since been seen.

He enjoyed no fresh food, he possessed no freeze-dried meals: and this before the age of refrigeration. Yet, with a cargo hold full of wild animals, and absent the aid of modern sanitation, he lost not a soul through hunger, scurvy, or disease. Minus the technological advantages of loran, radar, sonar, and sextant, without even a spyglass, he discovered land with the only navigational aid he had on board—a dove.

Then he ruined his perfect record and made the greatest blunder in the annals of seafaring. He ran aground on top of a mountain.

If the *Ark* is ever found, it will require high altitude gear rather than diving equipment to explore the ancient, hallowed remains: down parkas instead of rubber suits. The *Titanic* lies more than two miles deep, and can be reached only by specially constructed submersibles, or unmanned Remotely Operated Vehicles (ROVs); it will never be touched by human hands. The *Lusitania*, at a depth of 320 feet, has been dived by commercial divers wearing cumbersome and expensive oil rig apparatus, breathing a mixture of helium and oxygen, and tethered to a surface support vessel by means of umbilical hoses. Only a few divers in the world are qualified to operate at this depth.

Of history's four most renowned shipwrecks, only the *Andrea Doria* is within the grasp of conventional scuba.

The Grand Dame of the Sea has gone down in maritime chronicles as one of the most publicized, most talked about, and most remembered of peacetime shippping disasters. The collision should not have occurred, and the liner should not have sunk.

Since the *Andrea Doria* was designed with the most up-to-date knowledge of marine engineering, her owners claimed that her twenty-two watertight compartments made her virtually unsinkable. While this makes good advertising hype, those who know anything about ships readily agree that the word "unsinkable" does not apply to man's paltry creations. People have been more wary of this fact since the 1912 Titanic disaster in which two thirds of the complement of twenty-two hundred men, women, and children, perished.

On the night of July 25, 1956 after one hundred incident-free crossings of the Atlantic, Captain Piero Calamai drove his ship westward at nearly full speed through the fog-shrouded waters south of Nantucket. The bridge radar was in operation; it showed a blip representing a vessel sixteen miles away, but because of the liner's forward motion the relative movement of the oncoming intruder was not accurately determined.

After four thousand miles of uneventful travel from the luxury liner's home port, Genoa, the weary passengers quietly anticipated their morning arrival in New York. Their suitcases were already packed, and most of their luggage was stacked in the corridors or on the enclosed Promenade Deck, ready for disembarkation. Many people retired early. Silence pervaded the staterooms and public halls of the unsuspecting ship.

Earlier that same day a smaller and slower Swedish-American liner had left her berth in New York. The *Stockholm* now moved easterly on the first leg of a Scandanavian excursion. Only twelve hours underway, her passengers were just settling in, some still celebrating their first night at sea.

The officers of the *Stockholm* also observed a blip on their radar screen. Traveling under a crystal clear sky lighted by a full celestial panoply, they were not worried. They could not see the fog bank ahead; the blip could be nothing more than an itinerant fishing boat working a late night haul.

The watches of both bridges, however, initiated discretionary evasive maneuvers. An unfortunate chain of navigational decisions worsened a situation already dire. By the time the *Andrea Doria* steamed clear of the clinging mist, and the two ships became visible to each other, it was too late to avoid a collision.

Standing on the bridge wing of the *Andrea Doria*, Captain Calamai watched helplessly as the reinforced bow of the *Stockholm* pierced the hull of his ship and penetrated thirty feet through passageways and staterooms. The *Stockholm's* bow was shorn off; truncated steel girders scraped along the outer hull of the still charging *Andrea Doria*. Almost immediately, the *Stockholm's* broken stem fell out of the wreckage, leaving a terrible, gaping wound in the Italian liner's starboard side. The cold sea rushed in to fill the sudden void.

The *Andrea Doria* took an immediate list which increased perceptibly during the frantic, frightful hours. The collision bulkhead of the *Stockholm* retained its watertight integrity; the ship lay dead in the water as she lowered lifeboats to help her wounded sister. There followed a night of confusion and sorrow: confusion as the 1,650 passengers and crew of the *Andrea Doria* were forced to abandon ship; sorrow for the fifty-two people who lost their lives.

As the world watched, the magnificent Italian liner listed beyond help, taking on more water than her overworked pumps could eject. A small flotilla of rescue vessels, led by the crack French liner *Ile de France*, picked up survivors. After a valiant, eleven hour struggle, the most elegant liner of the Italian merchant marine heeled over completely and slid raucously beneath the waves. That frozen moment was 10:09 a.m., July 26, 1956.

On that day the *Andrea Doria* assumed new meaning.

She would not become as other ships: a forgotten, rusting hulk, lost in the dim memories of seafarers and insurance files. Banner headlines shouted her fate around the world. Contraversy surrounded the circumstances of the collision, and eventual sinking. The maritime community went into mourning—not only for the passing of a ship, but for the passing of an era.

The sinking of the *Andrea Doria* was the first stroke of the death knell of oceanic voyages. Airplanes were faster and safer, and were becoming cheaper: they were already cutting a sizeable slice of the corporate market, and they were beginning to dominate the tourist trade. The age of the jetsetter was aborning.

By her celebrated, if untimely, demise, the *Andrea Doria* avoided the humiliating fate of many of her contemporaries: the long ocean tow to third world scrap yards, to be torched apart and recast in everlasting obscurity. Instead, she still resides serenely in her last port of call: a beckoning Siren to those whose ears are unwaxed.

It is here that the life of the *Andrea Doria* actually began.

Sea anemones festoon a lonely lifeboat davit.

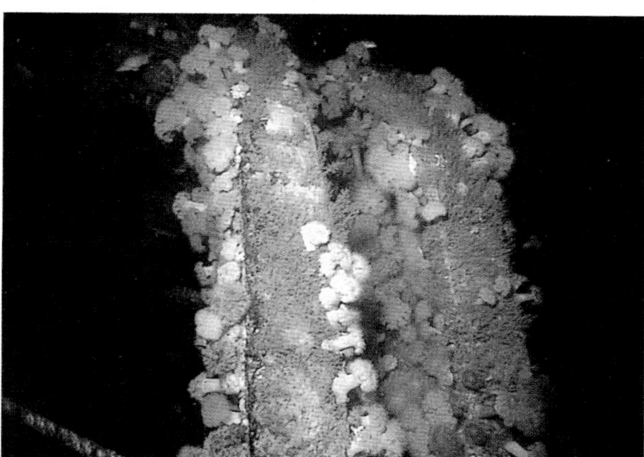

Side-scan sonar printout of the *Andrea Doria*.
Courtesy of Klein Associates.

Boat Deck window.

PART 1

CHALLENGE OF THE UNKNOWN

Courtesy of the Mariners Museum, Newport News, VA.

Because the *Andrea Doria* lies on her side, interior appointments are ninety degrees out of phase.
Top: Bathtub.
Right: Toilet.
Bottom: Stairwell and ornate railing.

CHAPTER 1
THE DREAMERS

"The free exploring mind of the individual human is the most valuable thing in the world."

—John Steinbeck

Andrea Doria art. Courtesy of the Italian Line.

The Dreamers

Men have always been dreamers.

Throughout recorded history there has consistently been a strain of men questing to go where none has gone before. He has trekked over lonely deserts, chopped through hostile jungles, climbed high mountains, endured the cold arctic wastes, and even ventured into the vastness of outer space. Despite the hardships, he is drawn like metal to a magnet by the challenge of the unknown.

The *Andrea Doria*, lying on a smooth sandy bottom in two hundred forty feet of salt water, instantly became a flung gauntlet.

The floating Italian palace represented a sizeable monetary enticement. Construction costs of hull and machinery amounted to $30 million. Furthermore, her sumptuous furnishings and prize works of art were worth, according to several estimates, an additional $10 million to $28 million.

The ship was an ocean going gallery of Italy's finest works of art, displaying, in part: a sixteen hundred square foot mural by Salvatore Fiume, covering eight walls; paintings by, Luzzati, Predonzani, Zuffi, Ratti, Bragalini, and Felicita Frai; marquetry by Beltrame and Rossi; copper relief by Calvetti; ceramics by Rui and Gambone, tapestry by Michael Rachlis. Public partitions were elegantly adorned with mosaics, frescoes, fabrics, crystals, and panels of rare woods. First Class staterooms were tastefully papered by artists such as Piero Fornasetti.

The luxury did not end here. In the middle of Fiume's Renaissance mural was a full sized bronze statue of the sixteenth century Admiral Andrea Doria for whom the ship was named. The sculptor Paganin portrayed the admiral in armor, posing with his sword. Donated by the admiral's descendant, the Marquis Giambattista Doria, was the original silver family crest that had once hung in the admiral's Genoese mansion.

Add to this such ponderables as the silver chalice and candlestick holders in the chapel, as well as other religious ornaments; reusable ship's fittings; the contents of a dozen safes spread throughout the vessel; and Chrysler Corporation's experimental automobile, the Norseman. The $100,000 sports car represented more than two years of engineering, design work, and construction. It was hand built by craftsmen at the Ghia plant in Turin, Italy.

There was also the miscellaneous cargo: $2 million worth of furniture, wines, woolens, silks, cottons, and olive oil; $25,000 of vermouth; five tons of provolone cheese; a shipment of industrial diamonds; and, if rumors are to be believed, a quarter million dollars in currency and jewels locked up in the First Class purser's safe.

The latter was probably the wildest dream of all. Tales of riches always abound following a tragedy where recovery seems impossible. Take, for example, the 1914 loss of the *Empress of Ireland* in the St. Lawrence Seaway. In that case, claims for loss against Canadian Pacific were so enormous that insurance underwriters decided to hire a commercial diving outfit to raise the purser's safe and return to the claimants their valuables, rather than to pay off in cash. The salvage operation, performed in one hundred fifty feet of cold, dark, silt-laden water, in a wreck lying on its side, was a masterly job of recovery: it is a story in itself. The safe was brought up by hardhat divers, sealed by government officials, and removed to a bank for safe keeping. Then, it was opened in the presence of the court, the claimants, and their legal representatives.

Imagine the surprise, and the shock, when it was discovered that the value of the jewels and money actually contained in the safe was worth less than five percent of the amount claimed. Such is the nature of human conduct, and out of such circumstances do rumors arise.

Little wonder, then, that such a large store of wealth lying within easy reach of the imagination brought so many salvage schemes to the surface. Italian naval Captain Alfredo Viola immediately proposed that for a mere $1.6 million, the *Andrea Doria* could be raised by the simple procedure of filling her with compressed air. As a marine construction expert for the Italian Ministry of Marine, his calculations that the 40,000 to 50,000 deadweight tons could be offset by 73,000 tons of buoyancy may have had some validity.

Other salvage experts felt differently. The expulsion of water from within the hull would significantly reduce the overall weight, but sealing off the innumerable portholes, hatches, ventilators, and open glass doorways, to say nothing of the cathedral-like collision hole in her side, would be an impracticable task for hardhat divers. Besides, ships are not designed to withstand internal pressures. Supporting members and cross beams that keep sea pressure out would not hold air pressure in.

True, the most successful salvor of all time, Ernest Cox, had raised dozens of sunken German destroyers, cruisers, and battleships sunk at Scapa Flow in 1919, using the compressed air method. But those were warships of heavy duty construction and strengthened with armor plate; they had been scuttled by the expedience of opening the sea cocks, so there was no external damage; and most had capsized, so the upside-down hulls could be filled like open ended bells. The wrecks were also much shallower. A ship lying on its side presented insurmountable problems. If anything, because of ballast in the keel, an inflated hull would have a tendency to right itself. The decks were not strong enough to hold in air: they would simply explode outward.

A spokesman for the Navy Salvage School said, "Salvaging cargo or machinery from that depth is doubtful, for it would be almost impossible to cut the hull with torches. The hull probably would have to be blown apart."

Many sunken vessels have been partially salvaged using this method. It was not uncommon in the old days to have divers lay explosive charges alongside a wreck's outer hull plates in order to peel them off. Once flenced like a dead whale, divers could then enter below deck compartments to recover valuables.

This method was utilized most recently in 1981, when saturation divers cut their way into the strongroom of the cruiser HMS *Edinburgh*, sunk in 800 feet of water in the Barents Sea.The incentive was $80 million dollars of gold bullion, which they succeeded in recovering. But the technology was twenty-five years after the sinking of the *Andrea Doria*.

As early as 1931, however, the P & O Line steamship *Egypt* was salvaged in a similar manner, from a depth of 370 feet, as was the Canadian-Australian Line steamer *Niagara* in 1941, from 432 feet. But instead of using divers breathing compressed air, the work was done by mechanical grabs and buckets directed by a man sitting comfortably at a pressure of one atmosphere inside a Davis Observation Chamber, known as the "iron duke." Again, the lure was gold bullion. In each of these cases, the wrecks were literally blasted apart in order the reach the storage compartments where the desired cargo was located.

The *Andrea Doria* had no such concentrations of "treasure" to make worthwhile a costly venture of this nature. Certainly, her machinery alone was not worth the expenditure of time and materials necessary for retrieval from such a depth. No parts of the hull or cargo had any extreme value. In order to make a profit, the ship must be raised intact, then refitted and returned to service. Even granting that it was technologically feasible, shipping circles estimated that the total cost of recovery and repair could cost twice as much as the value of the final product: it was cheaper and easier, and more certain, to build a new vessel from scratch.

Yet, imaginative, low-cost salvage schemes continued to pour in from the private sector. One of the most absurd plans suggested that the interior of the hull be filled with ping-pong balls until the wreck floated to the surface from the implanted buoyancy. Besides requiring the use of more ping-pong balls than have ever been manufactured in the history of the world, this idea ignored the certainty that the balls would be crushed flat by the pressure of more than eight atmospheres. This table tennis notion was quickly tabled.

Another fanciful salvage proposal provided the necessary lift by tying helium-filled balloons to the hull. First laughs are mitigated by the congizance that this would entail more than a couple million, gayly colored party balloons. Even so, the room sized, thick rubber inflatable containers (now more properly called liftbags, although they do not fit the usual perception of a "bag") would require attachment points. Clamps are out of the ques-

A stairwell on the Boat Deck.

tion. Drilling holes through the hull plating would be equivalent to raising your car off the ground by cables attached to eyebolts through the roof: the thin sheet metal would simply tear off. Besides, the number of balloons necessary to lift the weight of a vessel that displaces 29,000 tons of sea water, is enormous. It also ignores the extra pull required to break the suction of the sea bed. Finally, balloons expanded by the decreasing pressure as they neared the surface, would burst—as did this romantic concept. The anonymous jester should stick to raising toy boats from his bathtub.

A further outrageous conceit held that a huge cofferdam be placed around the wreck, the water pumped out, repairs made on the spot, and the ship gently floated as the sea was allowed to seep back inside the retaining walls. Again, this method is an extrapolation of previous accomplishments. In 1912, the U.S. battleship *Maine*, sunk in Havana Harbor in 1898, was salvaged this way. We should "remember the *Maine*", but also understand that it was only three hundred feet long, it lay in a protected harbor, and was so shallow that its upperworks were exposed at low tide. The armchair salvors lost another battle with reality.

Finally, in 1957, a more realistic if somewhat cumbersome plan was put forth by Armando Conti, president of the Trenton Beverage Company. He had enough faith in his own ideas to start a subsidiary he called the A.A.A. Salvage Company. He hired the engineering firm of Marque Marine, of Wyandotte, Michigan, to work out the details. Conti had come a long way since earning $8 a week as a coal miner: his entrepreneureal skills were a matter of record. But this was to be his first venture into the arena of marine salvage.

Therefore, he relied heavily on Richard Meyer, a former Naval lieutenant, who was president of the Marque Marine Company. That outfit had already raised several ore ships in the Great Lakes, including the 10,000 ton *City of Cleveland*, using a modified pontoon plan.

The traditional pontoon method has received much publicity over the years due to its success in recovering several sunken U.S. submarines, most notably the *S-51* (1925), the *S-4* (1927), and the *Squalus* (1939). In these long, laborious projects, divers using water jets tunneled through the mud and sand under each submarine. Cables were pulled through the tunnels. The pontoons were flooded and guided to their respective places on the bottom. Each length of cable then had a thirty-two-foot long, fourteen-foot wide steel cylinder attached to the ends. A series of these rigs straddled the wreck. Then the compressors that supplied the air for the digging nozzles slowly filled the pontoons until the weight of the submarine was offset. Explosive charges could rock the sub to free it from the suction. The *Squalus* had also lain at the same depth as the *Andrea Doria*; divers on that job breathed helium and oxygen to counter the effects of nitrogen narcosis. The main difference between a submarine and an ocean liner is that the submarine is *designed* to hold air under pressure. The earlier salvage jobs were successful largely because divers sealed the submarines' compartments, and forced out the water with air, thus adding greatly to the amount of buoyancy available.

In Conti's modified plan, he did not intend to use pontoons at all. Instead, he proposed to employ collapsible tanks developed by the U.S. Rubber Company as liquid storage and hauling containers. These Sealdbuoys were constructed of three-eights-inch corded rubber, with edges that could be folded over and clamped with steel bars. Each one measured fifty-two feet by fifteen: a giant toothpaste tube that could be lowered flat to the bottom, then later inflated after the connecting cables were woven through the liner's portholes. Furthermore, these two ton sacks were not intended to raise the hulk of the *Andrea Doria* all the way to the surface. They would only provide part of the lift. Mostly, they would help bring the ship to an even keel.

The bulk of the lifting capacity would come from two Great Lakes ore carriers bridged together like Paul Bunyon's catamaran. A cradle consisting of seventy 4-inch cables would be threaded under the liner's sleek hull. With this rigger's nightmare in place, the ore ships would be partially flooded. The slack would be taken out of the cables. Once taut, the ore ships would be pumped out. Their combined buoyancy would raise the *Andrea Doria* some ten feet off the bottom. She would then be towed in her sling toward the South Davis Shoal, eighteen miles away, until grounded, and the process repeated time and again until she rested in 125 feet. At that point hardhat divers would undertake the task of sealing off the wreck's openings with steel plates so air could be pumped in to help lighten the load. They might even patch the collision hole.

If this sounds like a montage of every salvage trick in the business, it probably is. The diagrams, lifting capacities, and time schedules appear reasonable on the drawing board. Drawn on a sheet of typing paper, the lines of the cat's cradle are an eighth-inch apart. In reality, the cables would be spaced every ten feet, and would have to be secured to two rolling ore carriers at the mercy of the wind and sea.

The computed expense of this hallucinatory episode was upwards of $4 million. The 67,000 feet of 4-inch cable alone could not be bought for less than a million dollars, to say nothing of the ninety Sealdbuoys. And labor does not come for love.

While Meyers' engineering figures may have been calculated with genius, Conti's return on investment estimates seem overly ingenuous. He intended to sell the *Andrea Doria* to a shipping line, to be put back into service. Barring this, he fancied the hulk alone was worth $9 million as scrap. With steel bringing only $40 a ton, salvage experts using simple arithmetic concurred that a $1 million value was more realistic.

Conti countered this estimate with a stunning and visionary marketing strategy: he would sell the wreck piecemeal to collectors of ocean liner memorabilia. The greatest potential source of revenue would be the proceeds from the sale of souvenirs such as restorable art treasures, nautical artifacts, and the more than 1,200 place settings of china, glassware, and silver service. It was even suggested that the bronze propellers, each having tonnage in the double digits, could be melted down and recast into mementoes such as cuff links, tie clips, and charms. The idea was charming, to say the least.

It is undoubtedly fortunate for Conti that his year long negotiations with the Societa D'Assicurazione, the insurance conglomerate that became the owner of the *Andrea Doria* according to the Italian Line's coverage contract, broke down. The Societa entertained more than a hundred offers for the salvage of the liner, but accepted none. Most would-be salvors wanted to share the costs of salvage. The Societa would not even approve the standard "no cure, no pay" agreement: it wanted cold, hard cash, no future involvement, and no liability. There were no such takers, and Conti was unable to attract investors.

In 1959, a less elaborate proposition arose, one which would make a stab at the quick, small buck, rather than at the long, uncertain millions. John Sherwood, chief diver for the A.A.A. Salvage Company, resigned from that outfit and struck out on his own. His goal was the mythical purser's safe and its chimerical fortune. The projected cost of a mere $70,000, against the possible rewards of cash and jewelry, had a better chance of enticing willing backers.

His method was one of absolute simplicity. Using scuba divers to perform peripatetic tasks such as survey work, line handling, and tool

A porthole with the glass intact.

carrying, helmet divers would do the more stationary jobs such as cutting off the main entry hatch, clearing debris, tending lines for the divers going inside, and opening the safe. If marine growth or corrosion balked the working of the safe's combination, the door could be torched off, or blown off with plastic explosives. Once inside, hardhat divers would open the drawers and remove the safety deposit boxes and their riches.

Sherwood spoke with great resolve, but never followed through with his plans.

Meanwhile, ideas for the total salvage of the wreck were still in the offing. Next on the treadmill was Lloyd Deir, a self-employed rigger, mechanic, and heavy equipment operator with no experience in major marine salvage. When he heard that a 21,000 ton tanker had run aground off the Maryland coast, and had broken in two, he promptly dropped his tools and embarked on a six month apprenticeship, at the end of which he and his cohorts towed into port the stern section and machinery spaces of the *African Queen*.

He accomplished on a shoestring budget what would have cost a commercial salvor a small fortune. Now, still high on the wings of that triumphant operation, he dreamt up an invention he thought would bring the *Andrea Doria* to the surface. Said Deir, "It will cost big money, but it will work. I'll stake my reputation on it."

The stakes he really needed were monetary. His dreams faded quickly as he woke up to the sad plight of the *African Queen*. When the tanker was put on the auction block, it should have netted at least a million dollars.

The ghostly railing of the Boat Deck.

Unbelievably, there were no bidders. Deir had to practically give away his prize. The revenue generated did not even cover expenses, much less pay his wages. The much needed capital for his *Andrea Doria* venture evaporated overnight.

Eventually, technology began to catch up with the *Andrea Doria.*

By 1963 a Massachesetts engineer invented and patented a system of raising sunken vessels by injecting them with plastic bubbles. William Watson did not dwell in the shades of ping-pong balls. At his Techcraft plant in Salem, where he manufactured plastic products, Watson developed a buoyant, closed cell foam by combining a resin with a catalyst of amine or peroxide.

To implement the process underwater required the use of divers. The liquid chemicals were pumped into a ship's hull down separate hoses and passed through a mixing nozzle. The diver directed the newly formed substance into the vessel's compartments where it solidified, forcing out the water and replacing it with caked foam. The final product had a consistency of soft plaster which, after the ship was towed into drydock, could be cut out with shovels or carved out with sharp instruments.

Although Watson got his idea while pondering over the plight of the *Andrea Doria*, he never utilized his invention on the liner.

A similar process developed in 1965 by the Danish engineer Karl Kroeyer was actually put into use on a sunken cattle carrier in the Persian Gulf. Kroeyer's plastic started out in the form of crystals. A boiler topside heated the powdered polystyrene, turning it into pearl-sized, air-filled bubbles with forty times the original volume. Special pumps forced the airy foam into the 2,000 ton *Al-Kuwait*. It took three months and 150 tons of polystyrene to raise the ship from a grave that was so shallow that the starboard hull protruded out of the water.

In two years, the Danes had so perfected the technique that they raised the *Martin S.*, a 3,080 ton motor vessel, from 114 feet of arctic water off the coast of Greenland.

The U.S. Navy was interested enough in the salvage of large hulls that not only did it have observers on the Danish job, but it awarded a contract to General Dynamics' Electric Boat Division, in Groton, Connecticut, to conduct a study of modern salvage methods.

But it was J. Philip Murphy, president of the Murphy Pacific Marine Salvage Company, of Emeryville, California, who pushed for a chemical solution toward the raising the *Andrea Doria*. As the head of one of the largest marine salvage companies in the United States, he had already raised a 2,600 ton vessel from sixty feet by using a urethane foam developed by the Olin Mathieson Chemical Corporation which, similar to Watson's foam, was manufactured within the hull of the wreck. Murphy's tests showed that the process would work just as well at 240 feet as it did at sixty. Yet, actuality did not follow his dream.

The year 1970 brought another innovation into the quest for the *Andrea Doria's* riches: the Yellow Submarine. Not the vessel of Beatles renown, this was the *Questar I*, a deep water submersible built by Jerry

The glass in the Promenade Deck windows is so encrusted with anemones that it is completely obscured.

Blanco of Deep Sea Techniques, Inc. When the yellow submarine was launched at Coney Island Creek on October 19, Blanco told interviewers that it was designed for the specific purpose of salvaging the famous liner. This may have been advertising hype, for the *Questar I* was never used for such a purpose. Unlike the popular song after which it was dubbed, Blanco's Yellow Submarine faded into anonymity.

Meanwhile, inspired by the plethora of salvage schemes then abounding, Michael Cushman and Roger Frechette, both of Massachusetts, were building their own one-man submarine—out of cement. (The Mafia was not involved.) Since Cushman and Frechette could not afford the high impact, light weight metals of the deep water submersibles, they opted for a molded hull of 4-inch thick stressed wooden frames, thickened by five laminations of 1/4-inch plywood, onto which was added a reinforcing steel mesh and 1-inch of ferro-cement. A 5/8-inch fiberglas coating added both sleekness and additional strength.

The *Scavanger* was twenty-one feet long. Attached to the main hull like a limpet was an eight-foot long steel module: a crowded compartment from which one man could manipulate remote control arms that could supposedly cut 4-inch steel plate at a depth of 300 feet. Jules Verne would have been proud. The launching was set for 1971. As a method of salvage, Cushman and Frechette intended to shove inflatable rubber bags through the *Andrea Doria's* portholes until she floated serenely to the surface. If anything ever came of this scheme, it was not reported.

Many things go full cycle. In this case, ping-pong balls were to play another round. Based on the principle of the table tennis version, the Pressurized Sphere Injector Buoyancy System (PSIBS) developed by the Denver, Colorado, based Cyclo Manufacturing Company consisted of 11-inch diameter inflatable polyethylene balls which were delivered to the internal spaces of a ship by a 12-inch pipe inserted by divers through openings in the hull. Jim Helbig, inventor of the system, said there was no depth limitation to the PSIBS.

While still aboard the salvage vessel, the spheres were pressured with air to a pressure equal to or slightly greater than that of the water pressure at the depth of the sunken vessel. For wrecks at extremely deep depths, helium could be used as a pressurizing medium. A ton of buoyancy was supplied by eighty spheres. When enough spheres were injected into the hull to offset the weight, the wreck would begin to rise. The adjustable, two-way pressurization valves vented automatically as the external pressure lowered during the wreck's ascent. The spheres were reusable.

Helbig used this system to raise a 2,400 ton barge from a depth of fifty feet in the Gulf of Mexico. Its application to the salvage of the *Andrea Doria's* hull seemed appropriate. But by 1971, the Grand Dame had been on the bottom for fifteen years. Her value as a vessel that could be refitted and returned to service was now more than ever, a pipe dream.

Consider: in 1942 it cost $4 million and took a year and a half to raise the burned out hulk of the *Normandie* from her dock-side grave in New York harbor; refitting was estimated to cost an additional $20 million. Sadly, the illustrious French liner was scrapped—she brought only $166,000. It takes money, too, to tear a vessel apart and convert her hull plates into workable steel. In the same regard, the *Andrea Doria* no longer warranted the expense of total hull salvage.

I have poked fun at notions and salvage schemes that stretch from the naive to the preposterous. But, in all fairness, this is a simple task with the vision of hindsight, and from the comfort of an armchair. If these somewhat fanciful enterprises never got off the ground, or under the water, it is not because those who conceived them did not allow their imaginations to run free.

Inventors, scientists, and entrepreneurs, in challenging the unknown, must accept the pitfalls of veering off the path of rightness. This is what exploration is all about, whether exploring the depths of the sea or the depths of the mind. Ideas must first be conceived before they can be tested. Most inventions, theories, and business endeavors do not survive the experimental stage. But without such daring conceptions the road to truth can never be discovered.

Despite the potholes along the way, there will always be men engaged in the search. If one thing can be said in their favor, they at least had the courage to dream.

Steve Gatto peers into the black abyss of the stern Foyer Deck.
Photo by Jon Hulburt.

Of the First Class Bar that once looked like the picture above (courtesy of the Italian Line) only the stools remain. Jon Hulburt photographed the author (at right) taking the bottom photograph.

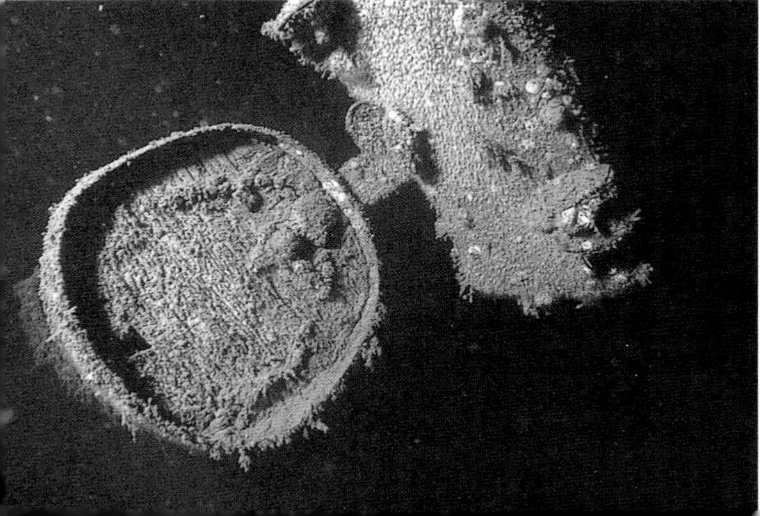

CHAPTER 2
THE SALVORS

"The only way you can assure yourself of limited success is to have unlimited dreams."

—Anonymous

A glass cocktail table photographed from three angles.

The Salvors

While some men only dream, others put dream to action.

No one ever mounted a campaign to salvage the hull of the *Andrea Doria* intact. But with less fanfare and more exertion than the drawing board sketchers, others designed salvage projects whose goals were more realistic: people who forsook their plush offices to don diving gear, who left their heated baths for the cold Atlantic, who tackled the task of underwater salvage with their own hands, who made no claims to glory other than what they actually accomplished.

The first of these visionary salvors were Glenn Garvin and Robert Solomon, two real estate businessmen from the nations capitol. Neither Garvin nor Solomon were divers themselves, nor did they know anything about marine salvage. But, they had valuable assets other than their own hard earned money for backing: they knew how to delegate work to those most capable of handling it.

With the courage of their convictions, they started out in 1963 by purchasing a surplus U.S. Coast Guard cutter from Jesse Simkins. He had bought the vessel from the Coast Guard and renamed her the *Top Cat*, after the famous cartoon character. The 125-foot cutter was fitted out in Norfolk, Virginia, where she was converted into a first class, do-anything salvage vessel. By the time she was completed, her decks were crowded with winches, motors, compressors, torches and cables, ropes and lines, a ten-ton hydraulic hoist, miscellaneous diving equipment, a recompression chamber, and a diving bell.

The bell was fabricated from a vertical steel tank cut in two, with the separated portions welded together with lengths of angle iron that left a space between the top and bottom. The lower section was filled with three tons of lead, the top was fitted with communications links, and could be charged with compressed air. It was like a large inverted drinking glass converted into an air chamber. The idea was to lower it to the hull so divers could pop up inside it and talk about the job at hand. It turned out to be too cumbersome, and was soon discarded.

At Simkins' recommendation, Dan Turner was hired to captain the *Top Cat*. Besides being a diver himself, Turner had long been a tug captain for Merritt-Chapman and Scott, which was then building the Chesapeake Bay Bridge-Tunnel. Turner was in overall charge of the crew submerging the tunnel sections of the twenty mile long causeway connecting Cape Charles with Cape Henry. With that job winding to a close, Turner accepted the new employment as captain, diver, and salvage coordinator of the *Top Cat*.

Along with Turner came his entire tug crew, including first mate Pee Wee Rose, his brother Pete Rose, and George Merchant, Turner's diving partner and right-hand man. Merchant was an explosives expert in the U.S. Navy. With the opportunity of a new job he rushed through his discharge.

The *Top Cat* left Hampton Roads in October, heading north on her first shake down cruise as a salvage vessel. On the eleventh, Merchant and another diver made the first exploratory dive on the *Andrea Doria*. With the lateness of the season, actual salvage was put off until the following summer.

The *Top Cat* spent the winter months in New Bedford, Massachussetts, and led a curious existance. Her crew took on any job that came up: light salvage, propeller changes, pier and hull inspections, and rescue and towing operations. But they never charged any money for their services. At the same time, they lived entirely on credit. Jack Saunders gave them fuel whenever they needed it, and he set up accounts for the purchase of groceries and drinks.

Meanwhile, Garvin and Solomon made several deals with respect to the *Andrea Doria*. Dow Chemical had some polymers, one of which was a styrofoam residue, for which it was trying to find uses. Company engineers thought the light weight polymers might raise sunken ships from the depths, and wanted the application tested. Life was looking for an exclusive story on the Italian liner; however, before they would put up any money, they wanted positive identification of the wreck.

It was not until the summer of 1964 that local divers were hired: Bill Dexter, Joe Paynotta, and Sal Zammitti. Their first job was to locate and identify the wreck. The *Top Cat* left her berth with high expectations, but for two days the boat rolled and pitched through stormy seas. Divers leaning over the rails were not looking for the wreck; they fought off seasickness with relentless abandon.

Finally, with George Merchant leading the charge, the divers donned wetsuits and tanks while Turner dropped a buoy on a wreck that offered a large fathometer recording. He maneuvered the *Top Cat* upcurrent of the float while his topside crew launched a motorized liferaft. Turner set a large, disposable anchor which the divers were to tie in as a permanent mooring line; the fifteen-man life raft was attached to the upper end, to act not just as a marker but as a working platform. It held tools, extra tanks, a compressor, a radio, and support personnel; a canopy kept the work crew dry from the spray and out of the direct heat of the sun. At all times divers were in the water, spare tanks and regulators were suspended from the raft as backup for decompression purposes. All dives were planned for no longer than fifteen minutes.

Braving turbulant seas, the divers rolled over the side of the boat and followed the buoy line down through the waves to where the water was cooler, calmer, and darker.

They got as deep as 205 feet before the line reversed its direction and curved back up: the result of too much slack. They pulled themselves upward until they saw before them the black hull of a massive ship. Zammitti later explained, "We came upon her from the wrong side. I could see the water line of the hull and a few portholes. In my heart I knew that this must be the *Andrea Doria*, but how in the world could I prove it? We must stay close to the descending line and yet, in any direction I looked there was nothing but a great expanse of barren hull, void of marine growth or fish life."

They terminated their dive, made a short decompression stop, and reentered the world of baleful clouds and choppy seas. Balked by worsening weather, the *Top Cat* faced fantail to the wind and headed for the safety of port. There she idled for three frustrating weeks.

When the *Top Cat* left New Bedford for her second trip, it was with a change in personnel: Lead diver George Merchant was now assisted by Joe Paynotta, Paul Harling, and Bob Laverdiere. The boat reached the Nantucket Shoals after a harrowing twelve hour journey, but sea conditions were too severe for diving. The *Top Cat* wallowed in the foamy troughs for two days before the weather moderated. Through the weeks of intervening storms the orange buoy marking the wreck site had miraculously survived.

Turner made a complete fathometer survey of the wreck. He judged the position of the bridge and dropped his anchor accordingly. Paynotta and Laverdiere dropped down the anchor line. They were rewarded with exceptionally clear water as they broke through the thermocline into the colder water surrounding the wreck. Said Paynotta, "I could see almost a hundred-foot section of ship, including part of the cargo deck, bridge, and boat deck." To their delight, the anchor lay only three feet from the wheelhouse doorway. Laverdiere tied in the buoy line he had dragged down, and they went off exploring. Paynotta regaled, "This had to be the *Andrea Doria*. Her size was awesome, with a graceful swept-back design of the latest jet airliner."

They stayed their prescribed fifteen minutes on the bottom, decompressed, then stood safety while Harling and Merchant went down. Harling described the wreck as "disturbingly noisy. There was constant clanging and banging of loose debris as it smashed against the bulkheads and deck. Occasionally I heard mysterious creaking and groaning noises from within the hull, as though the ship were still alive. The water rushing in and out of portholes and doorways made another eerie sound."

The pair inspected the bridgewing, pausing long enough to work loose the pelorus (sighting compass) from its gimbels. Harling tucked it under his arm. They dropped through the bridge door and descended into the gloom of the wheelhouse. All the bridge equipment lay at a ninety-degree angle on the vertical deck: a disorienting pictûre to a diver on the edge of nitrogen narcosis. They tied a locating line to the magnetic compass stand, with the intent of recovering it later. They, too, agreed that the wreck was that of the *Andrea Doria*. But *Life* wanted undeniable proof. The pelorus did not have traceable serial numbers.

The next morning brought perfect weather: a calm sea, a blue sky, and the warming radiation of the sun. Paynotta and Harling made the first dive of the day. They carried with them a 1,000 watt light to dispel the darkness of the wheelhouse. They spent their dive removing the bolts and electrical connections of the radar set. Just as they got it loose, the light shorted out and Paynotta ran out of air. They dropped the radar set on the horizontal outer bulkhead. Paynotta yanked his reserve pull rod, only to find that it was already down: he had no extra air. He charged up the anchor line and broke the surface almost unconscious. Pete Rose was the tender in the raft; he called Turner on the radio and told him to prepare the recompression chamber.

Harling was right behind Paynotta, ascending fast. Although he had enough air to make his in-water decompression, especially with the reserve supply dangling below the raft, he chose to stick with his buddy. Besides, once in use, the single door chamber could not be opened without total depressurization. If Harling later experienced symptoms of the bends, he could not gain access to the chamber without causing trouble for Paynotta.

Said Paynotta, "As I came aboard the *Top Cat* I could feel a slight but deepening pain in both shoulders and legs. I was beginning to feel the first effects of the bends." The crew stripped off his gear and rushed him into the onboard recompression chamber. Paynotta was recompressed, and treated by forty-five minutes of slow decompression. Afterwards, as he puffed on a cigarette, he complained of a lingering shoulder pain. He was put back in the narrow, tubular chamber, this time for seven cramped hours. He emerged hungry, but otherwise painfree.

It was not until late that afternoon, after they knew that Paynotta was all right, that Laverdiere and Merchant completed the job that Paynotta and Harling had set out to do. They tied a liftbag to the radar set and floated it to the surface. Now, at last, they had the proof they needed. The radar had been specially designed by the Decca Company; the label identified the unit as the one with which the *Andrea Doria* had been equipped.

Even so, the deal with *Life* ultimately fell through because of new and uncontracted demands. Instead of just documenting the salvage operation with a topside camera crew, the editors now wanted to send photographers down to the wreck to oversee the actual work. This required that each photographer be teamed up with an experienced diver, thus reducing the number of personnel available for working dives. Turner would not allow such a cumbersome and time consuming arrangement. *Life* was let go.

The next day brought a quickly descending fog for which the area is notorious. Not wanting to suffer the same fate as the liner now lying on the bottom, Turner slipped his mooring and drove the *Top Cat* slowly through the long Atlantic swells. Rain kept the men inside. The ex-cutter rocked and rolled with sickening irregularity.

Meanwhile, the men worked hard to readjust an underwater camera so that divers could maneuver it by hand. Harold Edgerton had designed the camera especially for deep water work; it was intended to be lowered by a cable, and, once activated, could take pictures at specified intervals. It was so heavy that even in the water its negative buoyancy was too much for a diver to handle. They removed as much extraneous metal as they could, and beefed up the housing with styrofoam.

The next day, in better weather, the camera was shackled to a safety rope and lowered to Merchant and Laverdiere, who were waiting for it on the descent line. As they struggled with the bulky housing, it got away from them. The camera plummeted to the bottom unattached. Merchant nose-dived after it. He followed the periodically discharging electronic flash unit right to the sand, hastily attached a liftbag to the framework, and sent the device back to the surface. Several exposures of the hull were obtained as the camera soared by, but further attempts to use the Edgerton camera were abandoned.

Instead, they relied upon a simple Nikonos 35-mm camera; illumination was supplied by the 1,000 watt light. Harry Leadbetter, a recent addition to the *Top Cat's* crew, added to his duties as engineer that of laboratory technician. He bought all the equipment he needed, and built a photo lab right on board. He processed the film and developed all prints during the dark hours of night.

The *Top Cat* divers spent a few more days acclimating to the depth by undertaking seemingly inconsequential tasks in light of what they were yet to accomplish. They recovered the port running light; they hacksawed off the floodlight that once shone down on the deck forward of the wheelhouse; they picked up a few souvenirs; and they tested the Dow Chemical polymers.

A surplus ammunition box stuffed with the styrofoam derivitive was taken down the descent line. At first, the buoyancy made the ammo box awkward. As the divers got deeper, it became more manageable. At a hundred feet, the polymer would not even support the weight of the thin steel container. When the styrofoam was scratched out of the box at the depth of the upper hull, and given an upward shove, the particles drifted toward the surface. Dow went on to search for other uses of the plastic residue.

The *Top Cat* returned to New Bedford for fuel, supplies, and an exchange of divers. Harling, Leverdiere, and Paynotta returned to their blue collar occupations. In their place came three U.S. Navy divers on leave from the salvage tender *Skylark*: Johhn Grich, Paul Heckert, and Dennis Morse. They were friends of Merchant from his time in the service; all were trained in hardhat and scuba.

Now work began in earnest on the main project which, in the mind of

Upper left (courtesy of the Italian Line) shows how it appeared after the sinking, with the windows overhead. Upper right shows how it appears to a diver looking up. Bottom shows the teak decking, nearly clean of marine growth. Opposite shows brass windows with the glass intact lying where they fell.

this author, goes down in diving history as one of the most incredible feats of underwater salvage ever accomplished on scuba. The goal was to recover the life-sized bronze statue of Admiral Andrea Doria (pronounced Andre′-a) from his stance in an alcove in the First Class Lounge.

Turner laid out the *Andrea Doria's* blueprints so everyone could study them. He carefully counted the lifeboat davits from the bridge aft, and determined where they would have to enter the hull in order to be above the alcove encircling the statue. The Promenade Deck was incased in glass that once protected passengers from the wind and the spray from the sea; the first chore was to blast out the framework that prevented access to the teak decked interior. The divers smashed out the glass and slung cables through the metal stanchions. The *Top Cat's* boom took up the slack. The blasting caps that set off the main charges were fired from the surface. Then the frames were hauled up to the deck of the salvage vessel. Kaleidoscopic oil patterns dotted the surface of the sea as blobs of fuel oil trapped inside the liner were set free by the blasts.

Dropping down to 185 feet, the divers next laid charges along the superstructure bulkheads separating the rectangular windows that lined the lounge. As each section was blasted free, it was hauled to the surface so the heavy metal fragments would not fall and possibly damage the statue, or later hamper raising operations. In this manner they kept blasting until they created an opening five feet high and eight feet wide.

Once the way was cleared, the divers descended into the Stygian blackness, dropped down to the centerline of the ship, and turned aft to face the alcove in which the Admiral was supposedly ensconced. Italian fabricators had done their job well: despite the *Andrea Doria's* position on her beam-ends, the Admiral still stood upon his pedestal; he now lay horizontally, like a sleeping soldier forever clothed in battle dress. he was 210 feet deep.

The four navy divers contined going down in round robin fashion, working in teams, and making two dives per day. The hours spent in floating decompression were long and wearisome.

They rigged double loops of three-eighth inch stainless steel cable around the statue by passing the end through the crotch, around the back, and choking it off around the neck, then out to a rope that was attached to liftbag that was inflated, but shackled to a lifeboat davit. The tension was taken up so that, once released from the pedastal, the statue could not fall into the bowels of the wreck. Turner was afraid that if he used explosives to blast the statue free from its mount, the detonation would damage the hollow casting. Electic torching was out of the question because of the voltage drop through the length of cable necessary to reach the work area.

The job had to be done by hand. Thus came the laborious task of cutting with hacksaws through the legs, and the rear support stanchions that held the bronze statue in place. The divers took turns sawing, sawing, and sawing. They broke several hacksaws in the process, and wore out or snapped all their blades. Turner was forced to run to the *Nantucket Lightship* for replacements. It was back breaking, arm wrenching work—but not a job they were about to give up. No one remembers how many dives it took to accomplish the task, but they all breathed a sigh of relief when the last cut was made and the statue swung free of the alcove. They left only the feet behind, having severed the statue above the ankles.

The weather was worsening. Turner knew that only a short time remained before he had to take the *Top Cat* to safety. It would be several days at least before he could return to the wreck to complete the job at hand. For Grich, Heckert, and Morse, their leave from the Navy had nearly expired. Rather than be left out of the denouement, and despite less-than-optimum diving conditions, they decided to go for it.

Turner put his ingenious lifting plan to work. While one team of divers gradually slacked the line holding the liftbag to the lifeboat davit, another team guided the 750 pound bronze statue out of the hole. Inch by inch the statue was allowed to rise up out of the Lounge, into the Promenade Deck, and through the upper window frame structure until it floated safely above the hull. The two-inch descending line was then detached from its mooring point on the wreck, and reattached to the cable sling around the statue.

The divers made their slow ascent. Surface conditions were so severe that they chose to complete their decompression aboard the *Top Cat*. It is Navy standard operating procedure to break decompression and dash into

Courtesy of the Italian Line.

a chamber before nitrogen bubbles in the bloodstream have time to expand, clot, and cause the bends.

Turner brought the *Top Cat* into position, retrieved his divers, and brought the descent line over the bow and took a bight around the capstan. He hauled on the rope until the thinner line, fastening the liftbag to the *Andrea Doria's* lifeboat davit, snapped. As the statue sprang upward, the capstan took in the slack. The air in the liftbag expanded at a prodigious rate, accelerating the ascent. When the liftbag leaped out of the water, the air dumped out of the open bottom. The statue swung like a pendulum to a position below the boat. The crane hoisted it onto the deck of the *Top Cat*.

After eight years of darkness, the Admiral almost winced in the glare of the sun.

What is told in a few short sentences required eight days of herculean effort, and the expertise of seasoned divers—to say nothing of the fiancial backing of two men who not only had a dream, but had the strength of mind to make it come true.

Garvin and Solomon set out to prove that divers with exceptional skill and experience could achieve spectacular results with limited resources. This they did admirably. A few proficient individuals are far more desirable than a work force of incompetents relying on millions of dollars worth of technology and an army of surface support personnel to make up for their deficiencies.

If Garvin and Solomon expected more of the limelight for their efforts, they were disappointed. They had put together a sleek, fast salvage vessel, a crack diving unit, and an capable and efficient captain and crew, and had proved that they could do what they set out to do. Every one of them should have received more media recognition for their accomplishment than they got.

The *Top Cat* dive team dissolved. With their leave over, Grich, Heckert, and Morse, returned to the navy and the *Skylark*. The boat worked its way south, eventually to jobs in the Gulf of Mexico where offshore oil exploration presented a challenge equally as difficult as underwater salvage. Turner and Merchant, as well as most of the topside crew, remained with the vessel.

For a while, the statue was the highlight of the National Social Club, on Union Street in New Bedford. When the *Top Cat* left for her new work station (after paying off her debts, including a $10,000 bar bill) she took the statue with her: a monument standing on the afterdeck where all comers could see it. Since Glenn Garvin had recently purchased the Sea Garden Hotel in Pompano Beach, Florida, he had a speical platform built for the statue in a second floor banquet hall that seated four hundred people. Two flights of stairs led patrons past either side of the magnificent bronze Admiral; they could not fail to see and appreciate it. Garvin called the banquet hall the Andrea Doria room.

Despite the public yawn in response to the *Top Cat* expedition, Garvin was unruffled. "I would do it again tomorrow. The experience was worth every penny of it."

Meanwhile, among a coterie of avid wreck divers, interest in the luxury liner remained intense. The reason most trips to the *Andrea Doria* failed to materialize was lack of funds. This problem was solved in a variety of ways, the cheapest being called the "charter." The first of these took place in June of 1966, when a group of east coast scuba divers, led by Michael de Camp, decided they wanted to see the wreck for themselves. (The following month, de Camp worked with Gimbel on a shark filming expedition off Montauk, NY, and the month after that he was part of Gimbel's tenth anniversary visit to the *Andrea Doria*; see Chapter 3.)

The distance to the site and the cost of hiring a vessel usually makes diving the *Andrea Doria* an expensive proposition. But thousands of fishermen go out on "head" boats every weekend, to chum for game fish or to drop their hooks on sunken shipwrecks. Overnight trips lasting two or three days are less common, but do occur: tile fish are found in water up to 600 feet deep; tuna trips frequently involve offshore trolling. What could be simpler, and cheaper, than chartering a head boat to take divers to the *Andrea Doria*? A dozen divers could split the cost twelve ways, enabling them to see for themselves the Grand Dame of the Sea. By this time, in fact, charter boats had already discovered the vast resources of cod and pollack that inhabited the sunken liner, and were already running overnight fishing trips to the site.

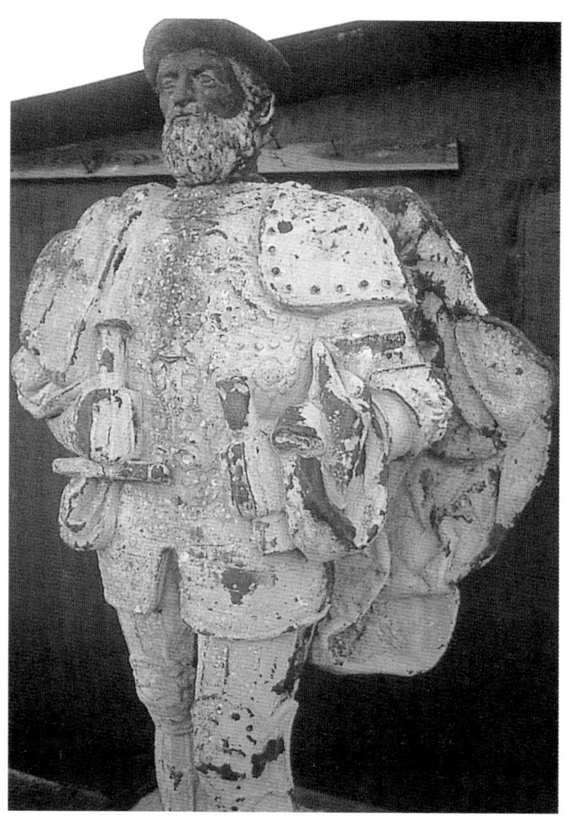

The statue and the feet as they appear today.

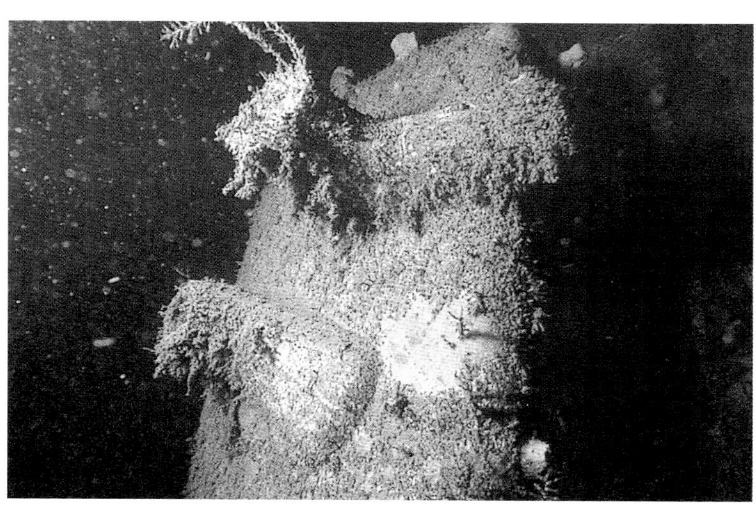

De Camp and his diving adventurers chartered the *Viking Starlight*. Because of the parameters set by scuba (limited air supply and in-water decompression), bottom time is usually limited to fifteen or twenty minutes. This may not seem long enough to explore a 700 foot long shipwreck, but these divers aspired to no goals other than to experience what the *Andrea Doria* had to offer.

On such a three day charter trip in 1967, John Dudas descended into the wheelhouse and brought up the binnacle cover and compass that the *Top Cat* divers originally intended to retrieve. In addition, Dudas' future wife, Evelyn Bartram, became the first woman to dive to the wreck of the *Andrea Doria*.

By 1968, great strides were being made toward more efficient diving

Below: John Dudas soon after recovering the magnetic compass from the *Andrea Doria's* wheelhouse. The cover kept it free from marine encrustation. (Courtesy of Evelyn Dudas.) Opposite: The compass and binnacle cover today.

on the famous liner. Alan Krasberg and Nick Zinkowski designed a two-man habitat that could be tethered to the high side of the wreck, and from which they could work while "saturated." Instead of decompressing after each dive, they would remain at depth for a week straight, thus saturating their tissues with inert gas; then, they would do one long decompression in the safety of their habitat after it was brought back up onto the deck of the salvage vessel. This would give them days, instead of minutes, to accomplish their aims: to cut through the ship's outer hull, sneak through the passageways to the purser's safe, burn off the doors, and remove the heaps of money and valuable jewelry stored there by wealthy passengers. After that, they would recover china and silverware to be auctioned off for additional profit.

Underwater habitats were not new, but so far they had been employed only for physiological experimentation; no one had yet used one to give divers more bottom time for salvage operations. Krasberg and Zinkowsky named their habitat the Early Bird. It was made out of wood.

This may seem like a step backward to the eighteen hundreds, the era of wooden diving bells, but in actuality this was no crackpot scheme. Krasberg was a physisist working for Westinghouse, and the inventor of the Krasberg Lung which the U.S. Navy found so useful. Besides being relatively inexpensive to build, the Early Bird's eight inch by twelve inch fir planking impregnated with polyester resin was supposed to provide more insulation than the standard metal chambers. Zinkowski was a Louisiana oil rig diver who gave credibility to the phrase "welders have hotter torches."

This uncomfortable workshop was ten feet long and four-and-a-half feet square. Surrounded by an assemblage of pressurized gas bottles, the habitat was supplied with helium and oxygen, a more reliable breathing medium than air in deep water, since it greatly reduces the anesthetizing effect that nitrogen has on the brain.

Although the expedition's primary purpose was salvage, photography entered the picture as a secondary aim. MGM backed the filming of a documentary to be entitled, with typical Hollywood burlesque, "The Great Underwater Wreck Robbery." Chief cinematographer was Al Giddings (still photographer on Bruno Vailati's photo expedition three months previously, and the only man on the trip with *Andrea Doria* experience; see Chapter 3); he chose as assistant cameramen Chuck Nicklin and Jack McKenney. In addition, *Life* assigned film maker Elgin Ciampi to "fly" a Pegasus diver propulsion vehicle over the hull in order to conduct a photogrammetric survey. Dimitri Rebikoff had designed the eight-foot-long wheeled sled with cameras mounted downward. The purpose was to take a large overlapping montage of pictures that could then be pieced together to form a detailed mosaic. Operating a second Pegasus unit was Jacques Mayol, breath-holding deep diving expert of world renown.

In all, three separate groups of divers operated off the steel-hulled catamaran *Atlantic Twin*. This was an amazing array of talent stuffed into a ninety foot boat. Yet, they were plagued with mechanical breakdowns almost from the very start. Even these adept masters were unable to overcome the difficulties conspiring against them.

The major problem was with the Early Bird. Construction and logistic delays postponed the launching until September; foul weather kept the expedition landlocked until October: not the optimum season for diving the Nantucket Shoals. Although it was pointed at each end to facilitate towing, a reasonably flat sea was necessary before the wooden habitat could be hitched to the stern of the *Atlantic Twin* and hauled to the wreck site.

Plowing through sheets of spray and pelting rain, the *Altantic Twin* finally left Newport, Rhode Island, on the third, dragging the Early Bird like a garbage barge. Sometimes, it was so inundated by the waves that it lay completely awash. When the boat reached the area of the *Andrea Doria*, the North Atlantic swells prevented anchoring the wreck. Large orange buoys were dropped on the bow and stern of the liner. The *Atlantic Twin* lay to on sand anchors off the wreck. During that first night a sudden squall and twelve foot waves nearly sank the Early Bird. The captain was forced to sever his anchor lines and head for the protection of Martha's Vineyard.

They returned the following day. Support divers, tethered to the *Atlantic Twin* by hoses that supplied them with heliox, attached mooring lines to the *Andrea Doria's* hull. The Early Bird was shackled to this open water elevator, and the lowering process began. The buoyancy of the air filled habitat was partially offset by a three-ton ballast platform in the middle of which was secured a manually operated winch. The support divers cranked the Early Bird downward, while the movie crew captured it on film. The habitat made it only partway when a mooring shackle pulled out of the wreck. The Early Bird shot to the surface in a great tangle of rope which would require massive rerigging.

Meanwhile, a brewing storm hit the Shoals with high winds and ten foot seas. The men sat it out for three grueling days. By that time, the buoy lines had become fouled and had to be cut free. Krasberg and Zinkowski dived down to the wreck and did the job themselves. Then more rigging was required on the Early Bird the following day. Giddings, Nicklin, and McKenney took the opportunity to film the wreck: Giddings with the camera, and Nicklin and McKenney with the movie lights. They shot fifteen minutes worth of stock footage.

The next day, they went down with Zinkowski so they could film him tying in the new mooring line and get more background material. This time, they were breathing trimix: specified proportions of helium, nitrogen, and oxygen. The divers were more clear-headed than when diving on air. They decompressed on oxygen, from bottles hung over the side of the boat.

After they came up, the *Life* team went down with their Pegasus machines. They had been working over the wreck but a short time when Ciampi's Pegasus died. Without mechanical propulsion it became a ponderous burden. Mayol cruised over to help. Ciampi tried to swim his machine up, but ran out of air at seventy feet. He inflated his vest, kicked frantically for the surface, and passed out.

The support crew had a Boston Whaler in the water. When Ciampi's unconscious body floated up in front of them, the alarm went out and the entire crew of the *Atlantic Twin* went into emergency mode. Mayol surfaced, too. He tried to save the machines by clipping them together, but they sank during the confusion.

Ciampi's still form was rolled into the Boston Whaler; Mayol climbed aboard with help. They were rushed back to the *Atlantic Twin*. Ciampi was carried into the recompression chamber still in his wetsuit, with Mayol right behind him. Krasberg jumped in with them, as tender. The door was closed and sealed, the chamber was quickly pressurized. Ciampi regained consciousness under treatment. Mayol was feeling no ill effects. Nevertheless, they decompressed in the chamber for seven hours. Neither one suffered residual affects from their ordeal and missed-stop decompression.

The weather turned for the worse. All the difficulties of getting the Early Bird to the bottom were aggravated. Almost overnight, the expedition fell apart. With both $40,000 Pegasus units lying somewhere on the bottom, the Life photographers were out of a job. With the habitat still bobbing around on the surface, the movie crew had no action to film. It was time for retreat. The trip was cancelled for the year, with the promise of returning the following summer. But, with its momentum broken, the forthcoming expedition never materialized.

The quest for the *Andrea Doria's* legendary safe lay fallow until 1973, when two ex-Navy divers founded a firm called Saturations Systems, Inc. Don Rodocker and Chris DeLucchi—with an impressive amount of experience in deep saturation diving—designed and built an underwater habitat that could be loaded onto a flatbed truck and transported anywhere in the country. Affectionately called Mother, it had a depth capability of six hundred feet, and could be tethered to the bottom from where the two divers could work for as long as twenty-one days. An umbilical cord to the surface provided breathing gas and telecommunications. In order to test the system, and to gain notoriety, they decided to cash in on the redoubtable media hype that followed any mention of the famous *Andrea Doria*: riding the waves of the air as well as those of the sea.

Mother. (Photo by Bill Campbell.)

Helping to back the operation was Bob Hollis (engineer, diver, dive shop owner, and founder of Oceanic Products) and his partner, machine shop owner John Clark. Both were primary divers, as well. Photographic documentation was provided by Bernie Campoli, Tim Kelly, and Jack McKenney. As support personnel there were back up divers, electricians, maintenance men, a doctor, and Rodocker's and DeLucchi's wives. Twenty-six people had to share one head and one shower.

The primary goal was—you guessed it—the purser's safe. By this time the value of the safe's contents had increased like a fish tale to over a million dollars—some sources reported as high as *five* million. But Rodocker and DeLucchi assigned a host of secondary objectives for exploration or recovery: several of the ship's banks, the wine room, the mail room, the captain's cabin, china and silverware, the chapel, the gift shop, the propellers, cargo, and cabin 172 in which was supposedly left valuable jewelry: a watch, a ring, and a broach, all with diamond insets. According to hand-written expedition notes, they also outlined a project the enter the generator room "via ventilator shaft forward of stack or thru bulkhead aft wall gift shop." This may sound grandiose, but anyone knowledgeable about shipwreck salvage knows that it pays to have alternate plans.

The 85-foot stern fishing trawler *Narragansett* was chartered for the trip. Crammed into its hold were scores of bottles of air, heliox, oxygen, nitrogen, and helium; as well as ropes, cables, electrical wire, and high pressure hose for pumping down breathing and torching gases. The deck was packed solid with diving equipment: a compressor for filling scuba tanks; a recompression chamber for emergency use by those divers using scuba; a welder for underwater cutting; a boiler to heat the water for the saturation divers' hot water suits; a push-pull compressor system that sucked breathing gas from the habitat, scrubbed it of carbon dioxide, and returned it for reuse; the eight foot long control van filled with electronics and valve assemblies, and from which the habitat and live-aboard divers were monitored; and Mother.

Although the habitat was surface-supplied with breathing mix, electrical power, heat, and cutting gas, should its umbilical connections be severed, it could maintain itself independantly for nearly a week. The lockout chamber was surrounded by gas bottles full of oxygen and helium. When tethered properly, closed circuit television kept the divers in constant communication with the support vessel. Mother was also designed to be towed in the open sea in anything less than a full gale.

The Saturation Systems campaign was the most expensive, most technological, most well thought out expedition to date. It was almost wiped out right in the beginning when a fifteen ton crane, loading equipment onto the *Narragansett's* afterdeck, rolled off the dock and crashed into the control van. Fortunately, the damage was slight. It took a day to move the crane and repair the van. The *Narragansett* finally left her dock in Fairhaven, Massachusetts, on July 22.

Onlookers gaze in awe at the massive coils of cable, stacks of compressed gas tanks, and the shark cage, waiting to be loaded onto the *Narragansett*. (Both courtesy of Bill Campbell.)

Trouble seemed attached to the inauspicious beginning. McKenney and Tom Ingersoll, a support diver, made the tie-in dive. But the grapnel pulled out before they reached the wreck, so their dive was aborted. Tim Kelly and Don Gay succeeded in securing the down line that afternoon; they tied in near the bridgewing, which was close to the double doors leading into the First Class Foyer, where the purser's safe was located. The next day, while setting up the permanent mooring line which would guide Mother to the wreck, DeLucchi discovered that they were tied into the stern wing instead of the main bridgewing: four hundred feet away from where they wanted to be.

It took two days to retrieve the lines and reanchor forward. Then the main mooring line chafed on sharp steel wreckage, and the *Narragansett* was cast adrift. Another day was lost resetting anchor lines before Mother was ready for her descent. No sooner did the habitat reach the *Andrea Doria's* overgrown hull than an electrical cable parted. Rodocker and DeLucchi were already saturated when they lost power. Rather than start out the job self-contained, they elected to return to port for permanent repairs. The ballast tanks were blown, and Mother was hoisted to the surface. The *Narragansett* was twenty-eight hours towing the habitat back to Fairhaven.

Mother was hauled out of the water with Rodocker and DeLucchi inside, under pressure, completing their decompression from saturation mode. The crane was still maneuvering the ten ton unit, jockeying for position, when the brake slipped. Mother crashed onto the dock. If the seals had been broken, the divers would have been killed almost instantly by explosive decompression. As it was, only Mother's undercarriage was damaged—and possibly some pride.

Saturation Systems was back to square one, without passing Go and without collecting $200. But Rodocker and DeLucchi did not give up. A week later found the expedition back underway, and the *Narragansett* moored over top of the *Andrea Doria*. However, their travails were not yet at an end. During the course of resetting the descent lines, a huge container ship ran right through the mooring buoys and sank one of them. If the *Narragansett*, or Mother, which was floating nearby, had been sitting on station, they would have been sent to the bottom as well.

Finally, on August 8, by running cables in one porthole and out another, Mother was latched onto the hull of the *Andrea Doria*. Rodocker and DeLucchi, with unlimited bottom time, swam out on their umbilicals and performed a cursory examination of the wreck. One of the first things they noticed was that the wheelhouse had disappeared. Although it had been there in 1967, when Dudas recovered the compass, now there was no sign of it. The light-weight aluminum structure, not designed to withstand the corrosion of the sea or the sideways pitch, had collapsed into the sand.

Now the serious work began. With torches out and the gas flowing, Rodocker and DeLucchi started lancing through the steel hull. Almost immediately, they were beset with a couple of minor problems. While they were working together on the hull, Mother, untended, began to flood. DeLucchi happened to glance toward the habitat and notice the gas leak. He rushed back and made compensating valve adjustments. DeLucchi also had several irritating cuts on his hands; once they became infected, he could not leave the habitat.

To ease the strain, Bob Hollis went into saturation. He helped Rodocker on the cutting while DeLucchi monitored Mother. Counting two days lost to broken welding cables, it took five days of shift work to burn a four foot square hole in the Foyer doors. By this time DeLucchi was able to enter the water, so he drew the lot of entering the black, tomblike interior.

Unexpectedly, he found complete disarray. Partitions were torn loose, but dangled precariously: they swayed like artistic mobiles, held together by pipes and wires. The drop ceiling was peeling away from its framework. Exposed conduits spanned haphazardly from deck to overhead. Thick electrical cables were woven through the hanging debris like the clutching strands of a spider web. DeLucchi groped through the rubble. Whenever he touched something, thick, obscuring swirls of silt billowed everywhere. Rotting wood and rusting metal was just waiting for the pressure needed to break it from its precarious perch.

DeLucchi got out. After discussing the situation among themselves and, through their communications link, with topside personnel, they decided to give it another stab. This time Rodocker went inside and DeLucchi tended the hoses.

Since the safe was on the starboard, or lower, side of the ship, Rodocker dropped straight down through the wreckage. Both divers were hooked up to the push-pull compressor by a common linkage. Rodocker's added depth created a pressure differential between his regulator and DeLucchi's. Water backed up into DeLucchi's face mask, nearly drowning him.

Rodocker called out in a heliox- induced Donald Duck voice that the bulkheads had "caved in." With DeLucchi struggling to keep his nose out of the water inside his flooded mask, the gurgling message reached the control van as "caving in." The topside crew thought Rodocker was being buried alive. They had no idea that it was DeLucchi who was in trouble.

Unable to communicate his trouble with his mouth underwater, DeLucchi did two things at once: while hauling up on Rodocker's umbilical with one hand, he opened his free flow valve with the other. Rodocker responded to the upward drag by ascending, although his weight made it difficult for him to rise quickly. When he finally poked his head out through the jagged opening, he saw his partner's difficulty, and disconnected his exhaust so DeLucchi could clear his mask of water.

On this sour note the expedition drew to a close: not because of the diving mishap, but because of the impracticability of reaching the purser's safe, or any other designated objective with the *Andrea Doria's* sweeping interior. When Rodocker passed the glass doors of the Gift Shop, still intact, he looked down and saw a pile of wreckage that covered the purser's safe under twenty feet of timber and miscellaneous rubbish. Removing it was an undertaking that Saturation Systems was not prepared to deal with. After spending eight days living in a twelve foot long cylinder not broad enough to stand up in, they called it quits.

For Rodocker and DeLucchi, at least, the quarter of a million dollars of investors' money was not wasted. They had set out to prove a system—that a saturation swat team was both feasible and cost effective. That goal they achieved. The *Andrea Doria's* riches did not come home in the *Narragansett's* coffers, but the real return on their investment was the knowledge that they could go anywhere, anytime, and do almost anything.

The *Andrea Doria* would reveal her treasures, but in a manner no one could have predicted. Sometimes, the best approach is oblique.

Some of Mother's interior controls. (Photo by Bill Campbell.)

Above and below: U.S. Coast Guard photographs depict the *Andrea Doria* in various stages of sinking. In the lower picture, the bow of the liner is already resting on the bottom. Opposite: press photographer Harry Trask captured the *Andrea Doria*'s last moments. (Courtesy of Harry Trask, the Boston Herald.)

CHAPTER 3 THE IMAGE MAKERS

"A photograph is not an accident—it is a concept."
—Ansel Adams

The final plunge. (Courtesy of Harry Trask, the Boston Herald.)

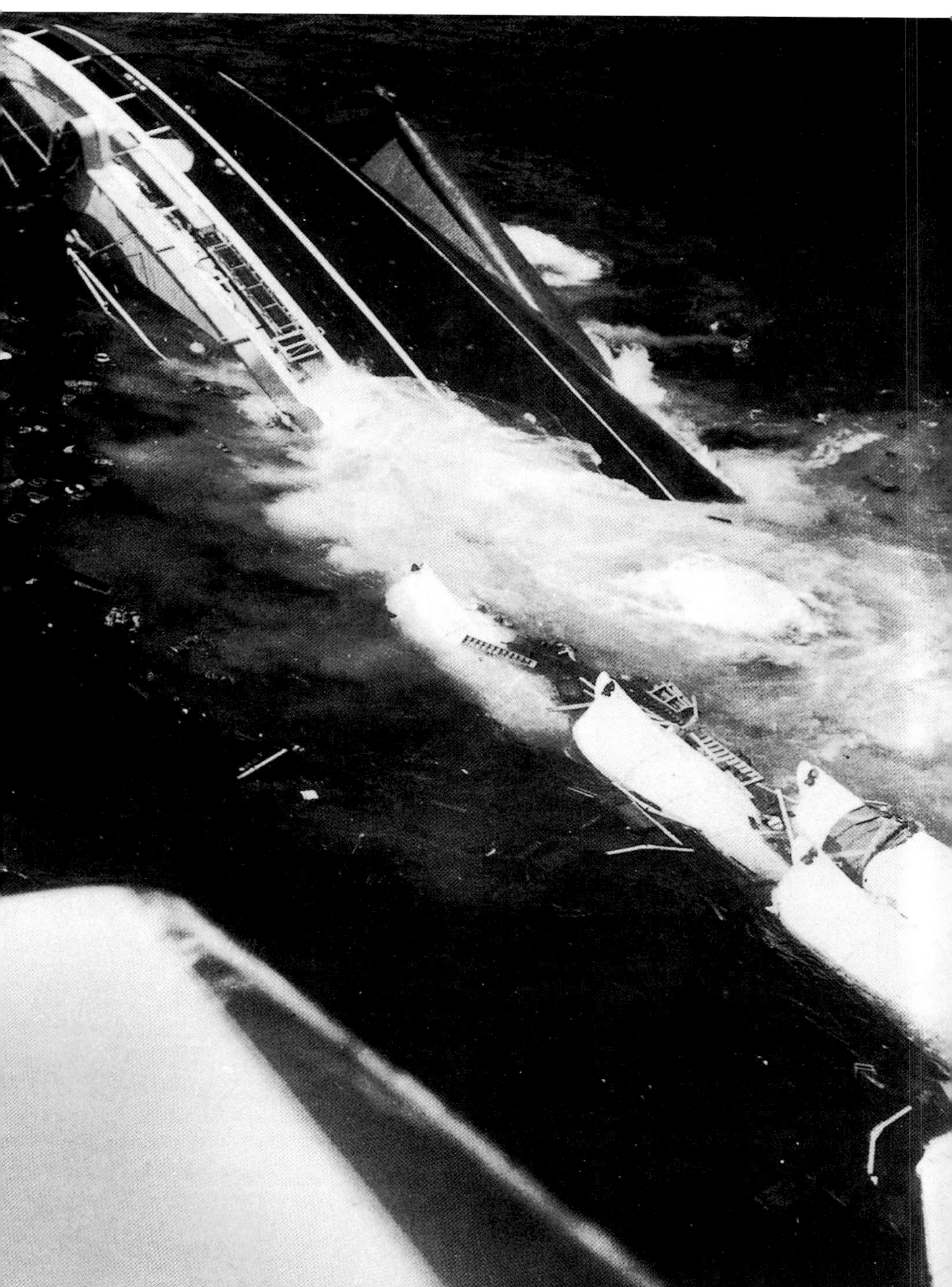

The Image Makers

The raked, sleek-hulled liner was still wallowing on the surface when the first picture takers clicked their shutters at her. As survivors rowed their lifeboats through the eerie summer darkness, toward waiting rescue vessels, anxious passengers crowded the rails to record the event. Despite the black of night, successful time exposures captured on film the awkward starboard list of the Grand Dame of the Sea.

By first light the sky was full of planes and helicopters: not just Coast Guard emergency craft, but flybys chartered by hungry news photographers eager to feed a starving public on images of the *Andrea Doria's* last gasp. The man who captured the magic moment most vividly was a staff photographer for the Boston Traveler (later the Boston Herald Traveler Corporation). His name was at that time obscure, but his series of aerial snapshots of the Italian liner disappearing beneath the waves won for Harry Trask the 1956 Pulitzer Prize for news photography.

Only twenty-eight hours later, Peter Gimbel and Joseph Fox became the first divers to see the *Andrea Doria* in what was to become known as her final resting place. At this time, Gimbel was an investment banker, a graduate of Yale where he had boxed and played freshman football. He was also an accomplished underwater photographer with many magazine credits to his name. Fox was a television script editor, with previous diving experience.

Gimbel called *Life* editor Kenneth MacLeish, who assured him that *Life* would purchase any underwater photographs that Gimbel might take of the sunken liner. Gimbel then hired a plane to fly him, his wife Mary, his twin brother David, Joseph Fox, and newspaperman Robert McKeon, to Nantucket Island. Gimbel knocked on doors for four hours, looking for a boat to charter. No one was interested in taking him to the site of the wreck; his offers were turned down time and time again. Finally, at midnight, he rang a doorbell that was answered by a man half the age of the old-timers who had scorned his proposal, and explained his plight. Captain Winthrop Ellis agreed to take him on.

At 4:00 a.m. Gimbel and his small crew loaded their gear onto the fishing trawler *Waleth*. That was when Gimbel discovered that the boat possessed no radio, no radar, no navigational equipment other than a non-functioning compass. It was too late to turn back; he was committed. Ellis cranked up the aged diesels, and motored the *Waleth* out of the harbor into a pea-soup fog. David stood on the bow of the boat and called out whenever he saw a channel buoy in the way. Once clear of the inlet, Ellis steered a course by dead reckoning. Eventually they left the fog bank behind, and that afternoon found them in the vicinity of the site some fifty miles south of the island. The spot was marked by an oil drum painted yellow, left by the Coast Guard. The normally dark blue ocean was blemished by an ugly slick of oil —the ship's diminishing lifeblood—while rising bubbles from the still breathing hull burst to the surface like crystal spheres.

Using double tanks with no pressure gauges, breathing off double-hose regulators, and wearing rubber exposure suits over woolen underwear, Gimbel and Fox dropped down the buoy line onto the gleaming, immaculate hull. Gimbel carried a 35-mm Leica camera with a 28-mm Canon lens, kept dry in an AKG case. He used black-and-white Tri-X film which in the processing laboratory was pushed to 1000 ASA. Gimbel had time to take only eight exposures when Fox signaled he was in trouble. He was suffering from carbon dioxide build up; he felt dizzy and uncoordinated. Gimbel inflated Fox's rescue pack, grabbed him by the arm, and rushed him to the surface. Fox recovered on the boat; the only aftereffect was a severe headache. Gimbel's quick action saved Fox's life.

Winnie Ellis again resorted to dead reckoning to get them back to Nantucket. Shortly after reentering the fog bank that still clung to the coast, the port engine ran out of fuel. With night coming on, Ellis anchored the *Waleth*. There was no way to call for help. In the light of morning, Ellis weighed anchor and let to boat drift in order to conserve his precious fuel supply. Later, he started the starboard engine and headed the boat toward shore. The *Waleth* ran completely out of fuel a quarter mile off Seasconset Beach.

Unperturbed, Gimbel jumped into the water and struck out for the sandy shore. He swam through the breakers with long, even strokes. Then, fins in hand, he walked along the beach until he found a private house with a telephone; the woman who owned it reluctantly let him use it. First he called MacLeish and explained the situation. Eager to get the film, MacLeish immediately dispatched two airplanes to rendevous with Gimbel on Nantucket; whichever one arrived first would take the film directly to *Life's* photo lab. *Then* Gimbel called the Coast Guard and asked for a tow for the *Waleth*.

Fog still clung to the island. Several hours later, airplane engines droned over the landing strip. The pilot made a daring instrument landing. Gimbel and his entourage (safely returned from the *Waleth*) boarded the plane and sped for New York. There they were met by two motorcycles. One driver snapped up the single roll of film like an anonymous contact in a spy film, and raced for *Life's* photo lab. Later, as the negatives were being processed, Gimbel called the technician on the telephone. Gimbel was concerned because he had had little time to bracket his shots for proper exposure. Over the wire the technician suddenly shouted, "We've got an image!" And Life had an exclusive.

Describing his experience on the wreck, Gimbel said, "The *Andrea Doria* is a stirring, unbelievable thing to see. She makes a tremendous impression because she seems so completely out of place. She seems almost alive."

Although he made only one dive on the *Andrea Doria*, for Gimbel that dive signified the beginning of a passion. When *Life* bought his photographs, he was hooked for life.

Life picked up at once on Gimbel's initiative. Assigning editor Kenneth MacLeish to the task, the magazine charged him with the responsibility of forming an expedition to the *Andrea Doria* in order to take color photographs for a later issue. MacLeish was a scuba diver himself; on a 1954 assignment he had descended to a depth of a mile and a half in Picard's bathyscaphe. He and Gimbel quickly organized a second trip. They hired three divers from the West Coast—Bob Dill, Earl Murray, and Ramsay Parks; Navy diving specialist Lieutenant Commander James Stark; and a fifty-foot, twin screw diesel cruiser out of Nantucket.

For three days in a row the crew faithfully left the dock and headed for the site of the *Andrea Doria*, only to be turned back each time by foul weather. On the fourth day, MacLeish chartered a plane and flew over the area where the wreck was supposed to be. The Coast Guard buoy had been carried away. Marking the spot was an oil slick half a mile wide and curving over the horizon. Even after the weather moderated, it took two frustrating days of running patterns with a depth recorder to locate the wreck.

Gimbel's camera this time was a Rolleimarin; artificial light was supplied by flash bulbs that imploded after use with a sound like a rifle crack. He faithfully recorded wooden handrails shining with varnish, still legible signs and plaques, the holystoned teak decking. On the projecting bridgewing the pelorus waited for an officer to take a sighting; in the wheelhouse the telegraphs and the helm stood loyally at their stations, awaiting orders.

Other than a thin film already covering exposed surfaces, the *Andrea Doria* appeared to be in pristine condition without gross damage or distortion: as if she had gracefully laid down to rest. MacLeish waxed poetic when he described his sensations: "Unscarred, seemingly impregnable, still equipped with every appurtenance of her impressive calling, this vast, intricate, luxurious human habitation lies empty and abandoned outside the world of men."

The divers limited their bottom time to fifteen minutes, swimming along the Boat Deck where only three weeks before passengers had walked. Parks commented on startling, booming sounds "due to the buckling of . . . the huge, steel plates" as the ship settled under her own massive weight, causing "the whole boat to shudder."

Because of the frightful weather, during the course of a week they managed to eke out only two more dives. For the last, they explored the stern area of the elegant ship. They found the glass doors to the bar and lounge closed, the panes uncracked; the tiles in the swimming pools were

A cross and a rosary in its case, recovered by the author.

clean and scrubbed. They swam through the glass enclosed Promenade Deck, where stacked suitcases awaited unloading and where the discarded shoes of survivors lay scattered about. Gimbel brought up one of the suitcases, full of rosaries, and returned it to its rightful owner, Mrs. Justine Messina.

The *Andrea Doria's* "brightwork still gleams, and the teakwood decks have not buckled or splintered. There is no flaking, blistering, peeling or rusting to be seen." However, one look through a stateroom porthole dispelled the illusion of seaworthiness, as "drowned curtains and mattresses and elegant furniture float in strange suspension." MacLeish found the interior in "violent disarray."

Meanwhile, extensive preparations begun only two days after the sinking were finally coming together. James Dugan, reporter and author of note, was slowly eating away at the logistical problems that so far conspired to delay the *Andrea Doria* Photo Survey. Most of the equipment, as well as the divers, had to be flown in from France. Frederic Dumas, co- director of "The Silent World", was the cinematographer. His cameraman was Louis Malle.

In addition there were backup divers, support personnel, a recompression chamber (which was rented to the *Life* expedition in the interim), compressors, and French diving equipment. Even after six weeks of frantic work, the expedition was held up for another week by the vagaries of Nantucket Shoal weather. It was not until September 13 that the diving tender *Samuel Jamieson*, loaded down with the latest electronic gear, left for the wreck site.

Dumas and Malle hit the water that afternoon. Malle carried the SM-3, a prototype 35-mm cinecamera. The purpose of the first dive was strictly reconnaissance: to shoot some test film at different lens openings in order to determine the proper exposure. They landed on the Promenade Deck and stayed only long enough to take their test shots. That night, Malle developed the exposed strip of film, and noted the correct aperture.

But that night a storm arose that blew them off the wreck. The *Samuel Jamieson* returned to port. During the six days waiting for the tempest to abate, the expedition subsequently lost its backup divers and support personnel due to other committments, its dive tender because of previously arranged charters, and all the electronic equipment which had been installed aboard. Dumas was fortunate enough to locate a sport fishing boat to take them back out: but it had no loran, no radar, and no room for the heavy recompression chamber.

When the *Striper* reached the site of the *Andrea Doria*, the marker buoy left the week before was nowhere to be seen. They had to start their search all over again. Late in the afternoon, Dumas dropped the grapnel on a fathometer recording, and it snagged. He and Malle made haste getting in the water to see where they were. They slid down the anchor line into water that grew darker with every deepening foot. At 215 feet they spotted the first sign of wreckage: the large blade of a propeller rising above them. They swam along the shaft never reaching the actual hull before they turned around in the realization that it was far too dark to produce an image on film.

Abruptly, the seven week expedition was over. Malle had burst an eardrum and would be unable to dive for several months. Dark clouds on the horizon presaged more inclement weather. The total accomplishment of nearly two months' work was twenty seconds of test film. As Dugan stated, it was "not enough to air."

Their lack of positive results is not an indictment of their ability, but a demonstration of the difficulties presented by the unpredictable water in which the *Andrea Doria* lies. The Italian luxury liner has stymied many skillful adventurers.

Dumas left with a negative impression that was not shared by Gimbel: "The sea owns the *Andrea Doria* now. She's a real wreck." Dumas never returned to the Grand Dame of the Sea. Gimbel could not be kept away.

August of 1957 found the intrepid explorer drawn back to the wreck. His partner this time was Ramsey Parks. During a week long excursion they managed only two dives through breaks in the weather.

No longer did the *Andrea Doria* appear trimmed for travel. Although she still wore her name proudly on the bow, her steel skin was coated with

The "D" in "Doria."

a thin veneer of marine growth. This living vegetation formed the basis of a new ecology. Attracted by the emerging supply of food, schools of cod, pollock, and jack swam graciously over her hull. The *Andrea Doria* was adapting to her new surroundings; the slow resurgence of life helped her blend into the natural scheme of things.

The top link of the food chain included the larger marine predators, with which Gimbel and Parks had a harrowing encounter. As the pair ascended the anchor line they were followed by a large blue shark. Their dilemma was evident: should they scramble for the safety of their support vessel, risking paralysis and possible death from the bends, or remain and confront the danger underwater? Both men drew knives. As the shark veered in too close for comfort, Gimbel stabbed it in the snout; his blade went in to the hilt. Although the knife evidently missed the brain, the shark swam away and did not return.

Gimbel got away, and *Life* got the photos.

About this time, Gimbel's brother David died of cancer. This caused Gimbel to reassess his own life. After deep introspection, he realized that he needed a purpose in life that was more fulfilling than business. He quit the investment firm and applied himself toward science, photography, and exploration. He returned to college for two years, studying zoology, physics, and mathematics at Columbia University, but could not find himself as a full fledged, bespectacled, laboratory scientist. He was too restless.

He became a trustee of both the New York Zoological Society and the American Museum of Natural History. He continued his pursuits in underwater photography. For Gimbel, life was moving in many directions. Together with G. Brooks Baekeland, he put together an expedition into the Peruvian wilderness known as Vilcabamba—an area never before visited by man. After an aerial survey, the team of four stalwart men parachuted into the jungle for what was planned as a two week exploration. They cut out a landing stip, but the moss covered ground proved to be too soft to permit the landing of their aircraft. They had to walk out; it took them eighty-nine days.

In 1964, Gimbel traveled to the ross Sea, in Antarctica, with the National Geographic Society. Under the charge of Carlton Ray, he dived under six feet of ice in the McMurdo Sound to film Weddell Seals in their natural habitat. Early in 1965, he and Bob Young filmed gray whales off San Diego. In June he produced, directed, and was the cameraman for a television film "In the World of Sharks," photographed off Montauk, New York. This was the testing ground for what he wanted to do with his life: make films.

It was not until 1966, after a nine year hiatus, that Gimbel returned to the *Andrea Doria*. His objective was to make a movie marking the tenth anniversary of her sinking. During a frustrating week and a half over the wreck he was constantly plagued with malfunctioning equipment and leaky underwater camera housings. Gimbel made nearly a dozen dives with veteran photographer Mike de Camp (see Chapter 2), but did not get enough footage for his proposed film. As he later recalled, "I was filming on a shoestring, and everything went wrong." Gimbel's time for success had not yet arrived.

A large blue shark thrashing the ocean to a froth in front of the author.

While Gimbel took time out, another man entered the arena.

Bruno Vailati was an Italian film producer and director. Among his many accomplishments was a television program entitled "Encyclopedia of the Sea." His purpose with respect to the *Andrea Doria* was to make a motion picture of the wreck as she lay on the bottom, becoming one with the sea. He would be burdened with a huge, housed 16-mm Arriflex movie camera, and a portable lighting system powered by a large battery pack carried on the back of his double tanks. From his home country he brought Stefano Carletti as his diving assistant; Mimi Dies and Arnaldo Mattei came as topside equipment handlers. Managing the still photography and sometimes shooting with a second movie camera was Al Giddings, then at the beginning of his dynamic career.

Vailati chartered the trawler *Narragansett*; the captain and two crew men took care of all the boat handling tasks. The boat was not anchored into the wreck at any time; instead, a buoy line was dropped, and each day the divers were ferried to the float in a Boston Whaler, and dropped off. When the dive was completed, the *Narragansett* returned with a shark cage dangling from her side. Once the divers entered the cage, the *Narragansett* drifted with the current until the hour-long decompression was completed. At night, the *Narragansett* anchored in the sand near the wreck, so she could make a quick retreat in the event of converging shipping traffic. More than one buoy was torn away during the *Narragansett's* absence.

The expedition left Nantucket on July 5. For the next three weeks this small band of men experienced all the setbacks proffered by the *Andrea Doria* to those who dare enter her realm. Storms rose suddenly, whipping the sea to a froth and creating huge waves that sent the expedition scurrying to port. Dense fog set in, making them cringe at the bellowing calls of approaching foghorns, or giving them tense moments as the *Narragansett* searched frantically for divers who floated unseen in the mist. Tide changes caused currents so strong that divers could not fight against them. And always, in the background, circled the silent blue sharks: majestic in their shimmering, turquoise coats, but meancing because of man's distorted notions about their ferocity.

But Vailati and his valiant men overcame all the obstacles thrust at them, and shot some unforgettable footage. They captured on film for the first time the awesome trawler nets draped over portions of the wreck like great, waving webs. Snagged in the coarse mesh were legions of ling, cod, and pollock: some struggled in the last gasp for life, others were ghastly remnants of torn meat and decaying flesh, a few were mere skeletons whose bones were barely held together by rotting ligaments.

The three man diving team explored the outer hull from stem to stern. They scraped the encrustation off the large brass letters that spelled out her name. They made three excursions into the bridge, filming telegraphs whose bells would ring no more, touching the helm which would no longer move. They created on film an elegant blend of the nobility and the eerieness with which the *Andrea Doria* is now imbued.

Al Giddings wrote with feeling and compassion, "She is a city once again, more populated now by ten thousand times than during her brief life as a great ocean liner. Sea anemones grow from her rails by the scores, and huge schools of fish of every type swim down her teak decked passageways."

"Fate of the *Andrea Doria*" is a classic film, not just because it was the first to accurately portray the Grand Dame in all her new-found splendor, but because it recorded her at an instant in time which can never be recaptured. Vailati, Carletti, and Giddings were the last to see her magnificent navigational bridge. The film is a lasting tribute to the ravages of the sea to which no manmade artifact is immune.

The film had its lighter moments, too, such as Carletti taking down a bagful of ping-pong balls that were crushed by the depth. The film incorporated pathos by showing a commemorative plaque placed on the bridgeworks. The film included fantasy, as any experienced diver knows that the depicted swim from fantail to bow, dragging cumbersome cameras, could never be made in eight minutes. Perhaps Vailati had reels of extra Promenade Deck footage he had to find a use for, and so spliced it together in a manner that would fool at least the amateur. To dispel confusion, the compass noted by Carletti—with the glass intact and the card pinned—was the gyrocompass repeater; Dudas had recovered the magnetic compass the year before.

Such is film making. What is important is that Vailati brought to the screen the images that most vividly interpreted what the *Andrea Doria* had become. He painted a picture of lasting beauty and serenity that reached out to people on a subliminal level, and made a statement that has validity for any shipwreck: do not remember me as I was, see me as I am. Change is the nature of the Universe.

Peter Gimbel was changing as well. As a cameraman, director, and film producer, he came of age with the vaulting success of "Blue Water, White Death," the critically acclaimed motion picture documentary about his worldwide search for the great white shark. This box office smash encouraged Xerox Corporation to fund Gimbel for the filming of a television special entitled "Mystery of the *Andrea Doria*."

Gimbel had long entertained a doubt that would not let him rest: why did the *Andrea Doria*, constructed in light of the most modern shipbuilding technology, list immediately to 18°, and within five minutes lurch over as far as 23°, when she was designed never to list more than 15°? This nagging thought formed a greater fascination for Elga Andersen, Gimbel's partner and co-producer of the film. Elga was a well known European actress among whose movie credits was "Le Mans," in which she co-starred with Steve McQueen, and "Elevator to the Scaffold," directed by Louis Malle. (The young cameraman who assisted Frederic Dumas on the *Andrea Doria* in 1956 went on to become a famous director in his own right.) Elga urged

Gimbel once said, "The sharks are the least of our worries. As neighbors go, they're not too bad," but he undoubtedly did not entertain that thought when Mike de Camp snapped this picture of him.

Gimbel to investigate the causes of the *Andrea Doria's* sinking. The unexplainable list provided the plot for the film. The year was 1975.

For diving support Gimbel employed International Underwater Contractors (IUC). This was the most fully equipped expedition to date, complete with a two-man submersible for reconnaissance work, an underwater bell as elevator and work station, and a crew of experienced commercial divers as assistants. Sharing the camera work with Gimbel was the redoubtable Al Giddings, veteran of the 1968 expeditions of Vailati, and of Krasberg and Zinkowski.

When dealing with the sea one must always fight adversity. The first days of August proved to be telling ones. The current across the wreck was so strong that the submersible did not have sufficient power to maneuver against it; it was retired after a trial effort.

Because of improper ballasting, the diving bell proved entirely unstable in the water. The original plan was to let the men ride it down to the wreck, then work out of it on umbilicals. This was similiar to the Saturation Systems method, except that the bell could not be tethered to the hull, and the divers would not be saturated: they would make hour long dives followed by five or six hours of decompression. But, during lowering and while hovering above the wreck, the bell swung and gyrated like a washing machine on a roller coaster; it had no delicate cycle. The bell was soon abandoned.

This forced the divers to surface jump on umbilicals that were fed down from the support vessel, the *G.W. Pierce*. The dynamic drag on the tether lines was incredible: the men returned from each dive exhausted from dragging their long umbilicals through the water, from fighting the current that pressed against the hoses, and from the long hours spent decompressing in the open sea. They did not give up, they just worked harder.

Two dives were made daily, one with Gimbel and one or two support divers, another with Giddings and his back up crew. They breathed tri-mix: a blend of nitrogen, helium, and oxygen. While modifications were made on the diving bell, Gimbel and Giddings started out with the external survey that was supposed to have been done by the submersible; They photographed the hull from the large brass letters on the bow to the sixteen ton port propeller. Plumose anemones now crowded each other for space, like waiting rush-hour commuters in a train concourse; hardly a spot of metal showed through the blossoming, feeding tentacles. The superstructure was veiled with more nets than ever, and they were still catching their grisly hawl of fish. Fifty-pound test monofilament grew like crab grass.

Because of the necessity of decompressing in the open water while hanging on to the anchor line, down time was kept to a minimum. Sufficiency of breathing gas was not a consideration since it was pumped down

A blue shark bounces its nose off the author's lens.

in neverending supply. The mixture was determined according to depth, with the divers going onto pure oxygen during the last stages of decompression. It was during this latter phase that Gimbel once went into convulsions due to too high a partial pressure of oxygen. Through the full face mask communication link, diving partner Ward Wright alerted the support crew of the problem. Gimbel was switched back to air while Wright aided him to the surface and to the boat's ladder. Gimbel, unconscious, was manhandled onto the deck and carried into the recompression. Gimbel revived, and recovered without ill effects. His close call did not stop him from diving.

Once the bell was ballasted with a five-ton anchor, making it more stable in the water, bottom time was increased to an hour. The bell still could not be used as a transfer capsule; it was lowered to a maximum depth of seventy feet, and parked. Now, at least, most of the required six-hour decompression could be completed in the relative comfort of the bell where the divers could get of the water and sit hunched over in cramped quarters. They either did their entire decompression in the bell, as it was raised gradually in order to lessen the pressure, or they did enough of it so the partial pressure of inert gas in the body reached an allowable tolerance that permitted the men to leave the water and dash into the on-board recompression chamber without fear of getting the bends during the short time at surface pressure.

Cold, induced by helium's high coefficient of heat loss, was a problem; but the use of tri-mix was considered appropriate because of the relief it offered from the effects of narcosis sometimes induced by breathing nitrogen-rich air when working hard at depth. The divers wore drysuits over several layers of thick woolen long johns.

Since the primary goal of the expedition was to find the answer to the rumor that internal damage to the *Andrea Doria* had been more extensive than previously thought, and that a watertight door aft of the compartment broached by the *Stockholm* may have been missing, thus flooding the main generator room as well, Gimbel and Giddings concentrated their efforts on getting into this portion of the wreck.

In alternating dives, they each entered number two cargo hold, forward of the bridge, and worked aft through the huge compartments. They went down three deck levels, then followed a sprinkler pipe. At one point they found hundreds of shoes and bottles of wine: part of a shipment intended for stateside commerce. At another they located a jaunty futuristic car which they decided must be Chrysler's "Norseman." Unfortunately, the disarray of twisted beams and broken bulkheads prevented further penetration.

Then, during bell decompression in rough seas, Giddings suffered a painful ruptured eardrum caused by the rapid pressure changes induced by excessive bobbing in the shallow depths, where the pressure differential is the greatest. He could not dive again until the perforations healed.

As Giddings rotated home and to medical facilities for treatment against infection, Jack McKenney was called in as his replacement. This was McKenney's third trip to the *Andrea Doria*, having first worked with Giddings on the Krasberg and Zinkowski project, then later helping to film the Saturation Systems salvage venture. Photographers of his caliber are not available on short notice; but Gimbel and Andersen had planned ahead by retaining him as a standby cameraman. His bags were already packed; he was on the next jet out of California.

McKenney was given brief instructions on equipment usage. The original idea was to penetrate the First Class Foyer using an Innerspace suit with a self contained rebreathing unit, but this proved to be unnecessary. McKenney dropped into the hole cut by Rodocker and DeLucchi in 1973. The Foyer Deck had cleared up since their earlier entry, and since my own excursion there in 1974 (see Chatper 4); most of the hanging cables and bulkheads had dropped away.

McKenney panned the interior with his movie camera, catching the still-intact glass doors that sealed off the Gift Shop, the staircase and ornate railing leading to the upper and lower decks, the patterns in the linoleum floor, a bathtub and sink, and, at the extreme bottom, a huge pile of rubble: the way to the impact area was again blocked.

Gimbel explored the exterior at sand level. Much to his chagrin, he found the bridge wreckage lying in a heap directly below its old location: a silent testamonial to the aging state of decay. This would have been an exciting discovery except that it blocked his entrance into the *Stockholm* intrusion spot. A fishing net was draped over most of it, but he was able to film some of the bridge controls as well as a lifeboat that had gone unlaunched at the time of the *Andrea Doria's* sinking. Stymied from further ingress, he conducted an examination of the bottom of the hull.

Then came an exciting revelation. Gimbel dropped over the curve of the bilge keel and descended along the ship's vertical flat bottom. Far lower down the liner's side than was ever suspected, he found the breach that had been made by the Stockholm's stem. The crack in the steel was two-and-a-half feet wide and twenty feet high. Gimbel crawled inside to the limit of his hoses; he passed through the ship's double hull, but was unable to go all the way to the number two cargo compartment. However, a broad, deep washout in the sand attested to the flow of water that must continually pass through the cargo hold and out the deep tank compartment: circumstantial evidence that the bulkhead in between had suffered massive damage. Even though Gimbel did not actually see this hole, it was the only viable interpretation for the gouging of the sea floor and the number of fish living inside. He was unable to prove that the door to the generator room was missing; but it was known that this room flooded immediately after the collision, knocking out power for the pumps.

In his mind, this last inconsistency still tugged. It lay dormant like a volcano waiting to erupt. The situation might have rested here in perpetuity had it not been for the incentive provided by the publication of a book in Sweden which sought to exact final retribution against the much maligned *Andrea Doria*. On the day that Peter Gimbel, at the tender age of fifty-two, ran the twenty-six mile cross-city trek in the New York marathon, there appeared in the *New York Times* a review of the book "The House of Brostrom: Portrait of a World Company," by Algot Mattson. Gimbel did not win the race—but he finished in three hours, twenty-six minutes, and fifteen seconds. When he arrived home, tired and sweaty, his sister Hope showed him the article.

Mattson, a Swede and a retired public relations man for Brostrom, contended that he had unearthed confidential correspondence between Italian shipbuilders and the *Andrea Doria's* owners, which described the bribing of government inspectors to overlook design faults in the liner's construction that made the vessel unseaworthy. Mattson also alleged that Italian government officials investigating the loss of the *Andrea Doria* conspired to hide these facts in order to prevent an international scandal. Brostrom was a Swedish shipping conglomerate; its subsidiary, the Swedish-American Line, owned the *Stockholm*.

The moment Gimbel put down the paper was the moment that "*Andrea Doria*: the Final Chapter" began. Elga Andersen, now Gimbel's wife, opposed another expedition to the sunken liner because of the oxygen hit Gimbel had suffered during the making of the 1975 film. The indefatigable Gimbel persisted. After six months of convincing argument, Elga gave in only because she saw that she could not prevent him from going ahead with the project. She agreed to help him: "As long as I can't keep you from doing it, I'll try to save you."

Backing was at first a problem because the television networks thought the venture was too risky. If the expedition failed in its aim to salvage a safe, and to prove or disprove the missing door hypothesis, they would be left with nothing. Instead, twelve partners, including Gimbel and Andersen, made a handshake deal to go ahead with the project.

The $1.5 million expedition left port on July 29, 1981, and stayed on its four point mooring over the *Andrea Doria* for thirty-three consecutive days. It weathered out Hurricane Dennis while the divers remained in saturation inside a chamber complex, one part of which could be detached and used to transport the men to the wreck. As in the Saturation Systems method, this obviated the need for decompression until the end of the job.

Gimbel and Elga, as co-leaders, chartered the 190-foot support vessel *Sea Level 11*, and contracted Oceaneering International (OI) and their team of commercial divers and crew. Steve Jennings was the diving supervisor; Ted Hess was lead diver. Two hundred fifty tons of equipment was welded to the deck of the *Sea Level 11*.

The main live-in chamber, called Mother, was twenty-three feet long and eight feet in diameter, complete with bunks, shower, and flush toilet. Connected to this was a transfer chamber that led both to a smaller pressurized chamber, and to the sealed bell that took the divers to their work stations. To offset the cold induced by heliox, the divers wore hot-water suits; water heated in an electric furnace was pumped to the divers through the umbilical hose, to wash continually over their bodies. Filming was done with Teledyne DBM9-1 16-mm, 400 foot coaxial load cameras.

This was a long way from Gimbel's first trip to the *Andrea Doria*, aboard a small fishing boat, when he wore a leaky exposure suit and shot black and white stills with a second hand Leica. Along with Gimbel as underwater cameramen were Jack McKenney, Bob Hollis (from the Saturation Systems trip), and Nick Caloyianis. Caloyianis drew the lot of topside backup: he made all his dives on scuba.

The *Sea Level 11* was set on a four point moor with four 3-ton anchors: two bow and two stern; this held the vessel in exactly the same spot over the wreck, and provided more stability than a single anchor. A down line was then attached from the boat to the wreck; this would be the guide line for the bell. The main umbilical that fed into the top of the bell furnished breathing gas, hot water, and voice communications; individual umbilicals from the bottom of the bell supplied these necessities to each diver.

The first team was pressed down: three OI divers to do the actual work, and McKenney as cameraman. After the divers rode the elevator to the wreck, one man stayed inside the bell to tend lines for the others. The primary job was to reach the First Class Foyer where the safe was located. Rodocker, DeLucchi, and Hollis had cut a hole in one of the Foyer Deck doors in 1973; Gimbel wanted all four doors completely removed. A large access was needed in order to carry out the interior projects. The two pairs of double doors were separated by a section of hull plate. Ted Hess cut through the framework using magnesium rods. Along with mechanical and weather delays, this task took two *weeks*.

One setback occurred when the downline tore loose. Gimbel and Hollis made a surface jump to reshackle the cable to the wreck. The dive went wrong right from the start: strong current swept their umbilicals into loops, the visibility was poor, and the men had trouble with their drysuits. They got tangled in surface lines as they were hurrying to get out of the ocean and into the recompression chamber. A crew member jumped in the water and cut them free, but also cut the line to which was attached a $10,000 Teledyne camera. It plummeted to the bottom. Luckily, three days later, McKenney found it in the superstructure wreckage.

Finally, cables attached to the *Sea Level 11's* crane lifted the doors out of the way, leaving an opening eight feet by twenty. Hess and McKenney went inside. Hess immediately found what he thought were the doors to the bank, or a teller booth window. McKenney, recording the operation on film, knew that they were the very doors to the Gift Shop that he had photographed in 1975. Because the topside monitor could communciate with only one diver at a time, while the other divers were isolated from the conversation, McKenney did not hear the dialogue between Hess and Jen-

The two people on the right are looking through the glass doors of the Gift Shop. Courtesy of the Italian Line.

nings. Hess smashed through the glass, only later to discover the truth of the situation.

Deeper down in the wreck, below the Gift Shop, lay a huge pile of debris: the wooden partitions, furniture, ceiling panels, and pipes and cables that had fallen away over the years. Neither the safe nor the bank was visible. Hollis realized that close measurements must be made in conjunction with the deck plans, in order to accurately locate the safe's position—hoping that it had not broken loose from its foundation, and plunged even deeper into the collection of trash.

Hess described the "giant mess" vividly when he declared in his helium-

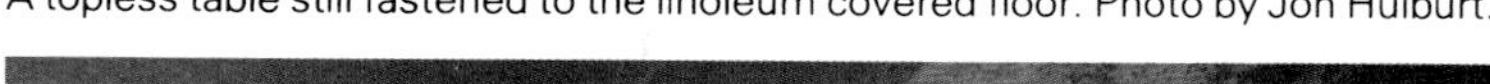

A topless table still fastened to the linoleum covered floor. Photo by Jon Hulburt.

induced squeaky voice, "It looks like somebody scooped up a big old house, dropped it from about a hundred feet, and came along with a bulldozer and shoved the whole damn thing in a cave."

Hollis pressed down to share the camera work with McKenney. Now two work-teams ventured out each day, one with each cameraman to record the events. The film eloquently describes the week-long process of clearing out the rubble, first using an airlift that sucked up only the small bits of wreckage, then trying a mechanical grab that did not work at all, and finally employing a large, steel mesh basket like an antique firewood carrier. Chunk by chunk, board by board, in practically zero visiblity, the divers dug through the silt and debris. They were spending five hours at a time, sometimes as much as eight hours, working inside the wreck.

After two weeks of saturation, McKenney started feeling the effects of the unnatural environment: earaches, skin rashes, a cold. He crawled into the small chamber for two lonely days of decompression. This left Hollis to film the laborious process of trash removal.

During this time, as the diving bell was being raised off the deck, the lifting cable broke. The four-ton bell slammed down hard, jarring those inside. If it had toppled off the deck, the umbilical hoses would have been sheared as the bell plunged into the depths. Those within would have died.

Another day the captain moved the boat without slacking the down lines: they snapped like rotten string. A day was lost rerigging. Then came two days of storms, accompanied by six to eight foot seas. The bell sat on the deck, unable to take the divers to work.

Morale was low. Allowable time was more than half over, with none of the objectives met. The crew needed new enthusiasm. Gimbel put Drew Ruddy into saturation because he thought the laid-back, church going commercial diver could infuse his companions with the spirit they needed. He did much more than that. While he was working at the bottom of the hole, Ruddy stuck his hand down through the rubble and felt a square, solid object. He cleaned it off and saw a handle and a dial. It was the Bank of Rome safe, right where it was supposed to be.

It was Gimbel's turn to take over the underwater camera work. He pressed down as Hollis came out of saturation. This left Elga to run the operation herself: one woman to supervise thirty men.

A few hours later, before work on the safe was even begun, the full force of Hurricane Dennis hit the Nantucket Shoals. For three days the *Sea Level 11* tossed around like a toy boat in a river rapids. The decks were often awash; loose crates and cables floated back and forth, crashing into the deck gear. A caroming barrel slashed the power cable to the port bow anchor winch; without power to maintain tension on the anchor, the line free-spooled and quickly covered the deck in a mass of anchor cable. The *Sea Level 11* was pushed by the force of the sea into the other three anchor lines. Because the *Sea Level 11* was top heavy from the weight of the saturation complex, she was in imminent danger of capsizing.

The men trapped inside the chamber felt the ship stop fighting. They immediately isolated the live-in chamber from the complex, and called for explosives. If the *Sea Level 11* sank, they wanted the chamber's welded legs blasted free of the deck. The divers could survive three days inside Mother. (Whether the chamber could be located on the ocean floor, and raised before the men died, was another story.)

Steve Jennings came to the rescue by disconnecting the electrical cable that powered the air compressor, and reconnecting it to the winch. The slack was quickly taken up, and the four-point mooring was re-established.

Another agonizing week was spent freeing the safe. Frequent halts due to torch cable problems, bad weather, and bell bouncing, frustrated the work schedule. Finally, Hess cut the safe off its mounts, and slung a cable around it. Camera in hand, Gimbel stayed inside the hole as the safe was winched out. Some 230 feet above him, the *Sea Level 11's* crane creaked and groaned with the strain. The tension mounted. In the most exciting live footage ever shot underwater, with the one-inch cable ricochetting off the steel sides of the opening, and the safe banging against the *Andrea Doria's* vertical deck, the two-ton mass was slowly hauled up from the depths. With each swing the safe threatened to pinch and sever Gimbel's life support cables; they would have parted like strands of wet spaghetti.

All these weeks, Caloyianis was making surface dives, on scuba, and breathing air, for additional photography when needed. Now, he and McKenney jumped in the water and filmed the safe as it reached the fifty foot level. The cables had slipped, and had to be repositioned before it could be brought out of the water. When all was set, Steve Jennings, both diving supervisor and job superintendent, activated the powerful hydraulics that finally pulled the safe from its watery abode and placed it safely on deck.

Phase one was accomplished, but at the cost of more than three quarters of the allotted expedition time. Hollis came out of saturation; this did not mean he stopped working. He joined Caloyianis and McKenney in making surface based exploratory dives for background footage. At the same time, Elga stunned everyone by donning scuba gear, going down to the wreck, and shaking hands with Gimbel on the broad, barnacled hull, thus becoming the second woman to dive the *Andrea Doria*.

Meanwhile, Gimbel charged into phase two without delay. The easiest way to reach the generator room was down a ventilator shaft. Because the upper superstructure decks had partially collapsed, and what remained was covered with trawler nets, the top of the shaft was closed off. Gimbel and Hess went back to the Foyer Deck and cut through the back wall of the Gift Shop. This put them into the ventilator shaft that ran right into the top of the generator room.

Together they penetrated deep into the *Andrea Doria's* interior. Yet, as soon as they entered the generator room they were stymied by an unanticipated barricade: a steel grate that was once a horizontal catwalk stretched across the top of the five generators. They could not find a way through. Reluctantly, they retreated. They had better luck on the next dive.

Dragging their umbilicals behind them, they squeezed through a stairwell leading into the lower level. Before them was a generator the size of a locomotive. They pressed forward through massive wreckage, to where the debatable watertight door should have been. As they swam along the twisted steel barrier, looking for a way through, they suddenly found themselves among the fish outside the ship.

A massive breach never before suspected led out to the sea. According to Hess, the hull was "split open like a ripe watermelon." The bulkhead separating the generator room from the deep tank compartment had been smashed open by the *Stockholm's* pivoting bow; the existance of the watertight door was incidental to the *Andrea Doria's* sinking. With three compartments torn open by the collision, the luxury liner had suffered a blow with which she had been unable to cope. The mystery of her sinking had at last been solved.

For the thirty men and one woman aboard the *Sea Level 11*, this was indeed the final chapter. But for Gimbel and Elga the saga was not yet over. The contents of the safe had yet to be revealed, and an hour and a half movie had to be condensed out of fifty-four hours of film.

A U.S. customs officer placed a seal on the safe shortly after the *Sea Level 11* motored into port. The safe was deposited in a shark tank at the New York Aquarium on Coney Island. There it sat until escaping bubbles alerted conservators that something was happening inside. The bubbles were analyzed, and found to contain methane: a byproduct of anaerobic bacteria. The safe was moved to a separate tank where the water temperature was maintained close to freezing: a bacteria inhibiting environment.

It was not until three years later, on August 16, 1984, when the film was aired on national television and transmitted via satellite to forty-two foreign countries, that the safe was opened and its contents divulged. The broadcast was the first live event special ever televised on a non-network station, and the first broadcast to beat all three major networks in the ratings.

Under the eyes of millions of expectant viewers, Gimbel's nightmare (that the safe might contain nothing but goo) was put to rest. Bundles of U.S. and Italian currency were found in a remarkable state of preservation after nearly three decades of sea water immersion. The rubber bands holding the money together still retained their elasticity. Also found were American Express travelers checks, and a leather pouch containing secret bank codes.

The country's foremost conservators spents many months treating and preserving the fragile paper. There were thousands of bills: the icing on the cake after a successful filming expedition. The actual monetary exchange value was unimportant, because as souvenir items the bills were worth much more. Each bill was individually embellished with its own design of deterioration, etched by the sea in which it had for so long resided. When they were put on sale, encased in plastic mounts, it became possible for anyone to possess a piece of the *Andrea Doria*.

What Jennings described as "a childhood dream" had come true. Yet, Elga admitted that one side of her wanted the safe kept closed so she could dream about what was inside: "It will be the end of a dream, and dreams are perfect."

To the adventurous, the end of one dream leads to another. Adventure follows adventure as we go through life pursuing our dreams.

Through his films, Gimbel has shared his dreams with the world. Now, for Gimbel, the adventure has ended. But the rest of us still have our dreams. We have Peter and Elga to thank for that.

Above: Lifeboat davits.

Below: Restored Italian currency.

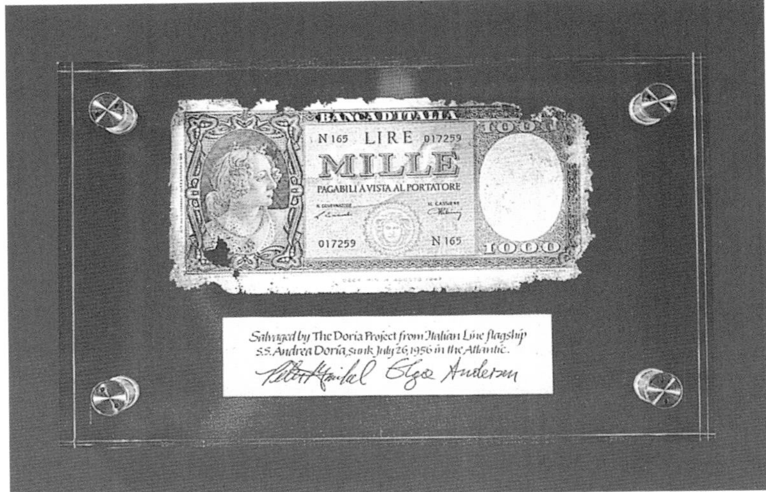

Below: Typical view of the interior.

PART 2

DIVE TO THE ULTIMATE

Marine life spotted over the wreck. Above: a mammoth finback whale.

A playful porpoise. Below: Minke whale.

CHAPTER 4
CHINA FINERY

''Experience is not what happens to you; it is what you do with what happens to you.''

—Aldous Huxley

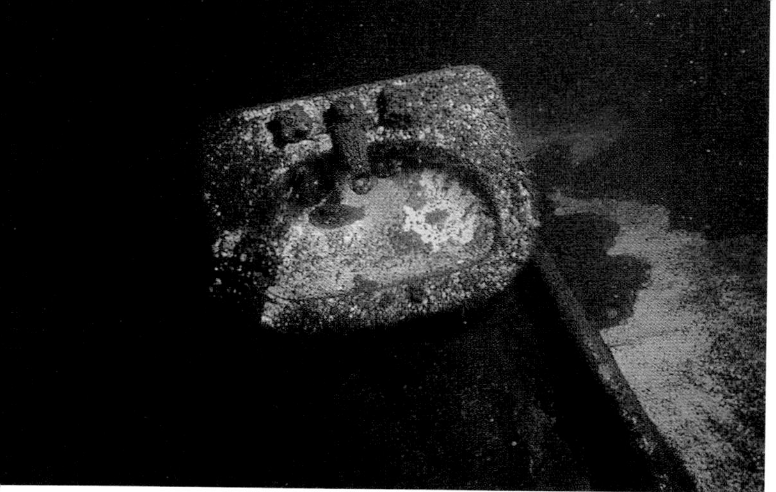

Inside only the fixtures are left hanging. Above: Sink.

Above: Bathtub. Below: Toilet.

China Finery

Suddenly she loomed in front of me: vast, impressive, and somewhat ominous. Without artificial light she came into sight while I was yet forty feet above her. Endless tiers of brass portholes, their glass overgrown with colorful, flowering sea anemones, extended the entire length and breadth of the hull, to the limit of visibility. There was no mistaking this massive steel structure for anything other than a sunken ocean liner.

One bridge wing protruded upward like the flipper of a playful porpoise. The Boat Deck railing was veneered with brown marine growth, although the teak armrest was clean and hardly aged. The boat davits stuck up like giant hooks: over the years they had snagged miles of monofilament and great trawling nets that were still catching prey—and were the bane of the unwary diver.

Beneath the superficial encrustation, and despite the structural failure of the upper decks, the vessel was easily recognizable as the *Andrea Doria*. I had studied photographs of her long enough to know.

When I took my dive certification course in 1970, I had never heard of the *Andrea Doria*. I had no fascination for the sea, no love of the ocean, no interest in either shipwrecks or history. I was not following a lifelong ambition. I was just escaping the humdrum existance that was a way of life in a peaceful and civilized country. I was restless, and needed some spark.

I went backpacking, mountain climbing, whitewater and wilderness canoeing, snowshoeing, winter camping, and skiing. I attacked diving with the same relentless enthusiasm, chasing adventure by diving deeper, staying longer, working harder, penetrating further.

One day on the boat, a dive buddy, chancing to see my battle scars as I pulled off my wetsuit, asked if my drive was a result of my Vietnam experience. The question stunned me: not because this was at a time when the topic of Vietnam was shunned by the American populace, but because in a flash of insight I realized that his not-too-casual reference was a perceptive analysis of my demeanor.

I flashed back to those long, torturous days spent in the jungle, suffering from the oppressive heat, insatiable insects, unbearable loads, hunger, thirst, aching muscles, and, of course, the onslaught of the enemy. Those experiences were so close in time that I still quivered when I heard the whupping blades of Huey gunships on maneuvers, still felt the chill of anticipation.

No sane person enjoys the horror of death and destruction, or cherishes war and killing. But the aftermath of combat leaves one in a state of mind that the ordinary citizen cannot, and can never, understand. One is never more alive than when one has survived a mortar attack, lived through a firefight, or breathes again after a sniper bullet has missed by inches. That is the time when one realizes how precious, and how fragile, life really is—and how meaningless it can become.

The terror of the moment soon passes, but it leaves in its wake the surge of adrenalin that itself becomes a goal. The post climactic feeling of discovery that one is still alive knows no bounds of joy. The continual reenactment provided by the endless field of battle flushes one with the type of excitement that explodes orgasmically, that leads to a kind of thrill that cannot be duplicated in everyday life. By its very nature it forces one to seek more of the same, like a nonfulfilling drug additon. As satisfaction becomes less intense, one tends to become nonchalant in the face of death: one lives only for that brief moment of pure, unadulterated gratification.

My lack of sensitivity to the mundane had turned diving into the stimulus for life. But my comprehension of that fact triggered the catharsis I needed. Understanding led to quiet self appraisal.

I did not seek close brushes with death, for that is foolish. I did not intend to charge blindly into inextricable circumstances. What I sought was personal challenge: to pit myself against the elements of nature, but in such a way that planning and forethought offered a strong measure of control.

This was the essential difference between walking point on a search and destroy mission, and plummeting into the depths of the unknown sea. Now I was in charge of my fate. I acquired the training, experience, and the best equipment and backup systems available—and tempered it all with judgment. I could back out any time the going got rough. I was in charge of my fate.

I first saw the *Andrea Doria* in 1974, when she was a Grand Dame indeed, particularly to my hopeful eyes. The trawler nets I perceived as a veil covered her face in bridal fashion. On her teak decks I imagined passengers still walking. But in reality she was falling apart. Her bridgeworks were gone, her stack had fallen off, her interior bulkheads were collapsing.

When I came across the jagged hole cut in the Foyer Deck doors by Saturation Systems the year before, I was drawn irrestistibly inside. I signaled my intent to my buddy John Starys, and dropped head first into the blackness. Starys maintained a safety position on the exterior. I inverted my body and sank feet first into the gloom.

With the great ship lying on her side I dropped parallel to the deck. To my left a naked steel bulkhead, having shed its protective paneling years before, rusted slowly in the stagnant water. I moved my hand lightly along the blue linoleum in front of me, steadying myself as I settled into the void.

Abruptly, the bulkhead ended. Stabbing my light at the darkness I studied the deteriorization. Pieces of ceiling tile clung to the suspension grid; a mass of conduits and electrical cables appeared to hold the loose framework togehter. My hand dislodged a frament of debris, knocking it downward into the black depths. I was overawed by the advanced state of devastation surrounding me.

A glance at my depth gauge showed that I had just passed the 200 foot mark. Peering down into the ebony abyss I was staggered by the tremendous pile of wreckage heaped on the bottom. The ceiling was bulged out, slowing obstructing further descent like the siphoning sides of an hour glass. I cringed as the rubble reached out for me, touching me: bits of wire and lengths of pipe. I fully concurred with Rodocker's and DeLucchi's opinion that the purser's safe was inaccessible. This was no place to be on scuba.

I inflated my suit and kicked urgently. It seemed like forever before my downward motion slowed, and stopped, and reversed itself. I felt the presence of wreckage leaning against me. Gradually, I worked my way upward through the jungle of debris. With my own stream of exhaust bubbles filling the chamber above, my light reflected back in my face. To either side I saw long lines of portholes. Gray light filtered through the openings, giving the room the appearance of a tomb. Enveloped in the vastness of this underwater vault, I felt insignificant.

A light glared in my face. On the other side of it Starys gave me the okay sign. Gladly I returned the signal. Outside, on the hull, I took a moment to catch my breath. The Foyer Deck was an eerie memory that haunted my dreams for eight years—until I saw Peter Gimbel's presentation on the recovery of the Bank of Rome safe.

With almost a thousand dives under my weight belt, and nearly two dozen on the *Andrea Doria*, the idea of yet another dive to the sunken liner no longer stimulated me. After half a dozen charters to the wreck the initial fascination had worn thin. What caused fresh blood to flow was the scene in Gimbel's film showing wine bottles and piles of dinnerware. I had recovered several souvenirs from the wreck, but the thought of having a dish with "Italia" inscribed on it was tantalizing. After the presentation I attended a party held at the home of Ruth Dugan—the widow of James Dugan, who had made arrangements for Dumas and Malle to dive the *Andrea Doria* in 1956. I talked with Gimbel and Caloyianis about the china; both were helpful in describing the route to the First Class Dining Room, as well as the conditions inside.

That winter I poured over the deck plans. The Dining Room did not appear to be a difficult penetration. It began about fifty feet aft of the Foyer Deck doors, at a depth of about 180 feet. Diving on scuba presented hardships Gimbel did not have: limited bottom time, open water decompression, hand-held lights instead of surface powered 1,000 watt Birn flood lamps, and, since they went in on umbilicals, no sure way back out of the wreck—but nothing insurmountable.

To optimize down time actually spent inside the wreck, and to afford a quick and easy return to the surface for decompression and unforseen emergencies, the dive boat had to be anchored right next to the Foyer opening with a permanent mooring. This meant sacrificing one or more dives to locate the entry point, not an easy task on a 700 foot long vessel encrusted with thirty-years-worth of marine growth and snagged fishing nets. It also meant I had to dive with someone I could trust.

Steve Gatto was such a man. He was competent, experienced, and self assured, and had packed an impressive amount of diving into three years. He had already made dives equivalent to our planned depth. This was his first trip to the *Andrea Doria*. His goal was to come back with a brass Promenade Deck window, but he was eager to help me locate the china first.

The charter boat we used was the *Sea Hunter*, Captain Sal Arena. When we left the dock in Montauk, on the eastern tip of Long Island, the weather was marginal. We took turns at the helm, steering a course for a hundred miles through lumpy seas. The forty-two foot wooden fishing boat could handle more than its passengers could, but if conditions got any worse the trip would have to be aborted.

As we arrived on site the preliminaries proved deceptively easy. I laid out the deck plans and showed Sal where we wanted to be. He dropped buoys at both ends of the wreck, estimated the location of the Foyer—about one third aft of the bow—and dropped a marker buoy. Steve and I jumped over the side dragging the anchor line behind us.

We alighted on the hull at 170 feet, I immediately recognized the graceful arch that designated the entrance to the Winter Garden. I spun around, swam a few feet, and was greeted by the yawning hole that led down into the Foyer. The wreck was a blur—I failed to notice the majesty and serenity of the Grand Dame of the Sea. Schools of fish and colorful sea anemones were blocked from my mind by profound intent of purpose.

I put my hands on the steel lip and peered down into the murky depths. I suppressed the urge to plunge right in after the china. That was not in the carefully laid out schedule. I shrugged off my enthusiasm and stuck doggedly to the plan. Only eight feet away a Pomenade Deck stanchion provided the perfect place to tie in. Steve pulled slack out of the line while I wrapped the steel cable around the metal support and secured it with a shackle.

A glance at my watch told me we had ten minutes to spare: time for a quick tour that would help familiarize Steve with the wreck while acclimating us to the depth and darkness. Dodging fishing lines, we dropped through the Promenade Deck window frames to 190 feet. Our deep diving experience proved its value: neither of us felt any effects of nitrogen narcosis. The ascent and thirty minute decompression went like clockwork.

Topside, things were not going so well. The weather forecast had been revised and thunderstorms were on the way. Rain posed no problem, but if the wind kicked up the ocean could become nasty. The Nantucket Shoals was no place to be when the barometer was dropping. Sal warned us that we might have to pull anchor and head for a lee shore that afternoon. In that case, we might weather out the storm in Nantucket. But if the front moving in proved too severe, or was predicted to last too long, previous charter obligations would leave no time to return to the wreck. The trip would be cancelled.

That possibility was a bad blow to all of us. Each person had his own reason for being here, each had expended much time, money, and effort to get to this point—not only in terms of his diving career, but in terms of the cost of the charter. Divers are always at the whim of the elements. It was the one eventuality against which we could not prepare.

In the chilly, clammy cabin we discussed the alternatives, while outside a squall swept by. Rain pelted the windows, waves slapped against the hull, solid sheets of water rushed across the deck and out the scuppers. Wave heights increased to three-to-five feet, white spume crested all around us. The boat rocked from side to side with a sickening, pounding motion. We needed energy, but no one felt like eating. Understated simply, we were very uncomfortable.

It seemed ironic that we should travel hundreds of miles through commuter traffic and roller-coaster ocean, only to be stymied a couple hundred feet short of our goal. To be assured of a second dive, we had to go in early. In these pre-decompression computer times I poured over the U.S. Navy Standard Air Decompression Tables: those ancient and often unreliable guidelines used to work out repetitive dives and decompression times. The short surface interval gave us a nineteen minute dive to a maximum depth of 190 feet as long as we were willing to spend forty-four minutes decompressing: nothing we had not done before. The proximity of the lode of china to the base of the down line offered the safety margin we needed.

Steve and I made a final equipment check. With the boat bobbing like a cork, the other dives helped us into our gear. We dropped into the frothy sea and kicked through rolling waves to the anchor line. At ten feet the water was much calmer. We double-checked our gauges, exchanged okay signs and nods, and turned head down into the depths.

My gut was twisted into a knot of apprehension: that was good, it would help keep me out of trouble. There is nothing like a little fear to keep one cautious. After all, the most important item I wanted to bring back—was me.

The surface water was warm and clear, but as we sank through successive thermoclines and layers of plankton, conditions worsened. The dark sky cut the amount of ambient light reaching the wreck. Gray turned to black, casting a somber cloak on the colossal hull. The rectangular Foyer Deck opening gaped like a monstrous mouth ready to swallow us.

Again we checked our gauges. Nothing is left to chance. We were in control of our destinies. There was nothing to hold us back but ourselves. We were psyched for it, but we both understood that at the least sign of difficulty the dive would be terminated. Neither would go ahead without the other's consent; either could call off the dive at any time. There was no room for argumentation. Steve enclosed a circle with thumb and forefinger; I returned the okay sign, and nodded.

I shone my light down the seemingly bottomless shaft; it revealed nothing but blackness. The adjacent deck showed the faint reddish hue of rusting steel, and an overall lack of contrast from the drab color of marine growth. Visibility inside was ten feet; fine particulate matter absorbed the artificial illumination.

With the ship lying on her side orientation was ninety degrees out of phase: the deck and overhead were vertical, the bulkheads horizontal. I dropped straight down, dragging one hand along the linoleum deck as I had done nine years before. On the other side, an access panel leered garishly from the remains of the drop ceiling. Broken pipes and a mass of cables fell out of the twisted gridwork, but most of the hanging debris was confined to a narrow layer close to the overhead. Compared to when I had been in here in 1974, it was as open as a cathedral. Oceaneering's divers had done a fantastic clean up job.

Straight down there were no reference points, just inky blackness extending beyond the beam of our lights. Swimming laterally as I sank downward I saw a ledge covered with debris: a counter top, chunks of wood, ripped up linoleum, and, oddly, a typewriter. The horizontal support was the side of the ventilator shaft, now the catchall for the partitions and contents of the rooms above. As we moved abreast into the gloom, the comfort of the opening fell behind. The light dimmed to a green pinpoint, and darkness became absolute. I was comforted by Steve's presence more than by his light.

The pounding in my ears was becoming more noticeable, a sure sign of added depth and narcosis. My apprehension increased. I concentrated harder and shrugged it off. We passed over a ceiling fixture whose glass shade was unbroken, then over a porthole storm cover with the handles dogged down. We left them untouched: we were looking for something far more exquisite.

A few thick cables hung across our path; we skirted them carefully. The debris thinned out until the horizontal bulkhead was uncovered. All too abruptly, the ledge came to an end. Ahead was an infinite chasm. Twin beams of light stabbed into the blackness, but could not reach any object. This was not the dining room.

Long hours spent studying the deck plans now paid off: I realized that we had gone the wrong way, and were staring at the void where the chapel used to be. I offered a silent prayer, and turned around.

At this point we had been inside the wreck for only three minutes, but it seemed like an eternity. We beat a retreat through the silt stirred up by our inward passage. Despite our best efforts to keep fin kicking to a minimum, our exhaust bubbles rising to the top of the corridor were dislodging rust particles from the overhead; it was descending around us like a thick, red snow.

In the worsening visibility we passed back over our waypoints: the storm cover, the brass fixture, the typewriter. When I recognized the gridwork in the Foyer and saw the access panel, I rolled over and looked up. Our entry point was there, but it looked so *small*. Yet, that postage stamp sized rectangle with the faint green glow brightened my heart immeasurably.

I glanced at my gauge panel to check the time and air remaining. We had wasted five minutes and were back at square one, but still had the opportunity to find the china. We agreed to keep going the other way. We passed over the ventilator shaft that Gimbel and Hess had penetrated during their historic dive through the ship and out the split bottom of the hull. The upended bulkhead was littered with rubble that had fallen from the overhead first class cabin: huge sheets of bathroom tile, broken pieces of porcelain from a toilet, wooden paneling, a red-backed chair, and broken fluorescent tubes.

Up ahead I saw a glimmer of white. My light zeroed in on it, then

waved back and forth rapidly to attract Steve's attention. It was the edge of a plate. We approached it with reverence. I touched it tentatively at first, then wiggled it out of the debris. It came free easily, but so did a swirl of thick mud. I beheld the gold leaf trim and the crown logo; the word "Italia" stood out.

At the same time Steve picked up a cut glass goblet etched with the same imprint. Another plate lay five feet ahead: an apple on a stick that drew us deeper into the bowels of the once luxurious liner. We glided over a lip, then across an opening that spanned the width of the corridor. Looking down I could see the ornate railing of a stairwell spiraling into the blackness. Like a car on a dusty road, we had to keep moving just to stay ahead of the silt.

I hardly had time to wonder about the diminishing visibility when we struck a bonanza: portions of china protruded from the mud as in a discarded junk pile. Dinner plates, cups and saucers, bowls, condiment dishes, and pie plates stuck out everywhere. The rims were gold plated, and some pieces depicted an Oriental design.

Before I touched a single piece of china I brought my gauge panel in front of my face mask and glanced at the dials. I put it down, muddled, then picked it up again. I had not understood what any of the gauges read. I recognized narcosis and knew that it was imperative not just for my eyes to see but for my brain to comprehend. I took another look, longer this time, and concentrated.

We were fourteen minutes into the dive, which meant that we had to be out of the corridor and starting up the anchor line in five minutes. I had a thousand pounds of air in my tanks—one third of what I had started out with: less than expected, but within acceptible limits. It was the depth gauge that shocked me: the needle was just shy of the 205 foot mark. No wonder I was feeling the effects of narcosis, and using more air than anticipated. I knew we had to hurry.

The mesh bag hanging from its wrist lanyard was enveloped in the swirling muck; I could not see it. I located the metal hoop by feel, unclipped it, and put my first precious plate inside. Then, before it was obscured by the charging cloud of silt, I set about picking up whatever was within reach. It was a free-for-all, or a gigantic garage sale in which everything was there for the taking. I did not pause to see what was going into the bag, I just worked as fast as I could. A bump on the shoulder, or a faint glimmer of light, was my only awareness that Steve was still there next to me.

All too quickly it ended. We had moved completely over the pile of china, and now I saw nothing but chairs and table tops. We had made one pass at the china. There was more, but it was veiled by churned up black ooze. Steve and I exchanged grins and thumbs up.

We turned and rose slightly to get into clear water. The heavy mud clung to the first few feet of the bottom. I dragged my hand along the linoleum floor to my left and kicked slowly toward the entrance hole, now seventy-five feet away.

Instead of seeing light ahead, I banged into a solid steel bulkhead.

For a moment I knew sheer terror. Frantically, I felt around me. There was rusted steel on three sides, as if I had swum into a closet—or a tomb.

I fought off panic, forcing myself to calm down and reason out the situation. Although we tend to forget it, the diver's world is three dimensional. When I pushed upward against the unresisting steel, my body was forced down. My fingers groped under a rounded lip. I ducked under and saw that the way ahead was clear. Coming in, crawling along the bottom of the corridor, we had passed beneath a bulkhead without knowing.

On the other side, a bathtub clung precariously to the vertical deck. Above it was a toilet and a sink. I passed through the remains of a first class cabin; all the partitions had fallen away, leaving only a few skeletal studs and the bathroom fixtures. Overhead, green dots of light that were cabin ports pointed the way out.

All photos on this page were taken by Steve Gatto.

Above: Chairs signify the end of the china. Left: Steve Gatto decompressing with his bag of china.

The weight of the china was taking its toll on me. I put air into my drysuit to take off the strain, but I still had to kick furiously to reach the elongated opening. By the time I swam through it I was gasping. As I took a moment to regain my breath, I felt secure in the knowledge that now there was nothing more than 170 feet of water between me and safety.

When I turned to check on Steve, he was not there.

I slipped the mesh bag off my wrist and placed it on the anemone covered hull. When I dropped back inside I saw Steve's light: he was struggling with his own bag of china; he had been much more efficient than I in filling up on goodies. I swam down next to him, took hold of the arm that carried the bag, and helped him to the upper hull. Grabbing my bag on the fly—there was not a moment to lose—I chugged toward the anchor line.

We headed for the surface with agonizing leisure, keeping to the prescribed rate of ascent. Steve halted at forty feet. I stopped below him. He fumbled with his white plastic writing slate, juggling his position on the line while hanging onto his heavy bag. As a precaution, he had written the decompression requirements for exceptional exposure. He made a quick calculation.

The seas were pounding relentlessly. On the boat, tanks, gear, and people were crashing around on the slippery deck. Everything had to be lashed down with rope. Underwater, we were being jerked around like subway strap hangers on a rough stretch of track. With the deep swells and ponderous waves, maintaining the proper stage for decompression was next to impossible.

Steve was unable to hold the slate still long enough for me to read the figures. He took his pencil and circled the "56": our new decompression time. Since I could not make out the times or incremental depths, I relied on his lead. I rose when he rose.

We were still at the thirty foot stop when he indicated his air gauge and drew his mitted finger across his throat. He was low on air. I looked at my own gauge and nodded. My main tanks were nearly empty, so I spat out the regulator and switched to my back up, a small pony bottle with an additional twenty cubic feet of air. Steve did the same. The current and rough conditions made it impossible to properly control my breathing rate: I was fighting too hard to hang onto the anchor line.

The spare bottle that was supposed to be hanging was nowhere to be seen. Sal had already pulled it up. He was in fear for the boat, and was prepared to cut free and head for shore as soon as Steve and I climbed aboard. A diver was stationed on the bow, watching our bubbles and ready to sever the anchor line with a sharp knife.

I tried hard to conserve my remaining air supply. My arms and shoulder joints ached from the constant wrenching motion of the anchor line. More than once the wildly gyrating line was jerked from my hand.

We still had ten minutes to go at the ten foot stage when Steve signalled that he was leaving. I offered to buddy breath with him, but he shook his head when I held out my regulator. He left before I could argue, or hold him back.

With tears in my eyes I knew that he was sacrificing himself for me. Within minutes he could be lying on the deck crippled with the bends, or paralyzed with pain or numbness, but he chose that alternative rather than taking some of my precious air and possibly putting both of us in the same predicament. I did not want to be saved at that price, but we both understood that it made no sense to have two casualties. Every minute, every second, remaining at depth decreased the chance of getting hit. I sucked gently on my mouthpiece.

Steve disappeared into the churning waves. I was alone with my thoughts, with my fears, breathing shallowly and deeply, exhaling slowly, hoping I could make my own air supply last—and praying that the safety factors we had built into our dive and decompression schedule would allow Steve to escape injury. The dive had run away from us, offset by variables either unconsidered or out of our control. Silently, I cursed myself for failing him.

I had stretched the envelope once too often, perhaps too far.

Something splashed above me. I looked up and saw Steve, coming back with another hastily donned set of tanks on his back. Another tank crashed into the water, tied to the boat by a thick nylon rope. Steve dragged it down to me. Steve had spent such a short interval unpressurized that the nitrogen in solution in his body had not had time to form obstructing bubbles in his bloodstream. Commercial divers often leave the water undecompressed, then are immediately repressurized in a deck chamber where they can complete their decompression penalty in comfort. The system works because their bodies are recompressed before bubble formation.

I was overjoyed to see that Steve was all right. He had saved the day. With a renewed air supply, we extended our decompression time as an added safety factor. A quarter hour later we both climbed on board the *Sea Hunter*, tired, relieved, and ecstatic about our accomplishment.

The anchor line was severed, Sal got the boat underway, and we swung around for a safe port of call. Our fellow divers gathered around to praise our booty—prizes that we would share with them all. Steve complained whimsically that he never got to tour the wreck, and did not get a window. His first visit to the *Andrea Doria* was quite an episode.

Had the venture been worth it? Yes. Would I do it again? Readily. As long as I controlled the odds with planning and forethought, as long as I built safety factors into my calculations, deep diving remained more design than chance. Unforeseen events were inescapable. But that is what life is all about. It is the challenge that makes life worth living.

In any situation fear is short lived, but the euphoria of that moment of escape lives on foreover.

Above left: Steve Gatto with his first found prizes.
Above right: Cocktail glass.
Below: The author's azaleas provide a backdrop for cups and saucers.

The author has revisited the china area many times, with other dive buddies. Opposite top: Jon Hulburt has just plucked a stack of patterned saucers from the mud, and prepares to place them in his goody bag, as the author moves in to take a close up (opposite middle). Notice the partially buried cups. Opposite bottom: Hank Keatts carefully digs through the mud. The U-shaped orange trombone slides are rusty dish holders that once kept the plates and saucers stacked neatly. Above: John Lachenmeyer racks up decompression time. Below: Sugar bowl.

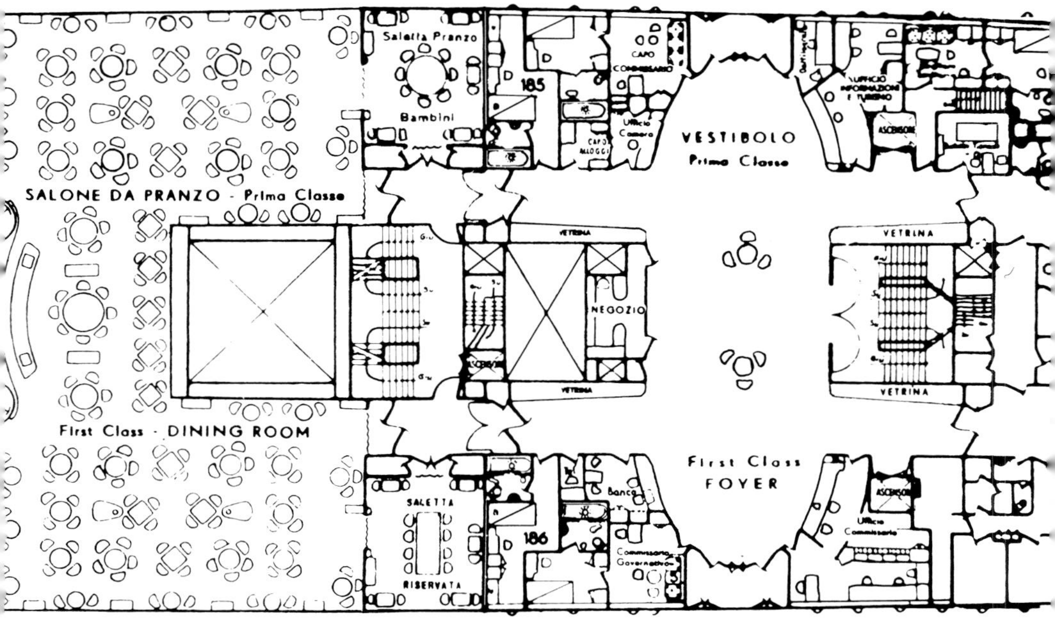

Saletta Pranzo
Bambini
185
CAPO COMMISSARIO
Ufficio Camera
CAPO ALLOGGI
VESTIBOLO
Prima Classe
UFFICIO INFORMAZIONI E TURISMO
ASCENSORE
SALONE DA PRANZO - Prima Classe
VETRINA
NEGOZIO
VETRINA
VETRINA
VETRINA
First Class - DINING ROOM
SALETTA
RISERVATA
186
Banco
Commissario Governativo
First Class
FOYER
ASCENSORE
Ufficio Commissario

Above: Original Foyer Deck plans. Below: The way it looks today. The china closets depicted in the lower drawing were put in to show how the china came to rest where it was found. The closets, along with most of the partitions, have long since fallen away. Soon, the ventilators will collapse and leave nothing but a huge empty hull and a deep debris field.

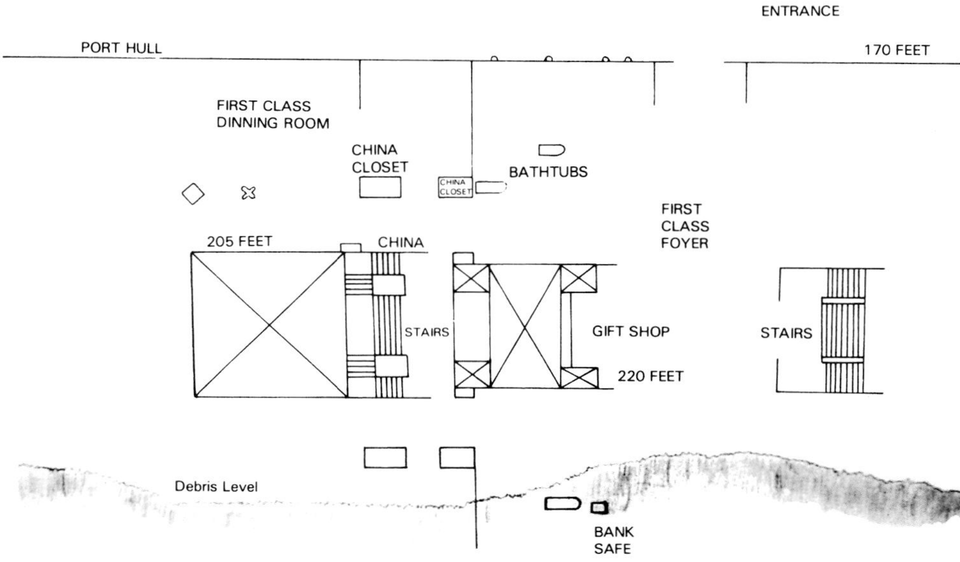

CHAPTER 5
A TOUCH OF CLASS

"In order to attain the impossible one must attempt the absurd."

—Miguel de Unamuno y Jugo

ITALIA

ITALIA

A Touch of Class

Some people still believe that because the *Andrea Doria* was worth some $40 million when she sank, she is worth that much today. This is no more true than saying that a $10,000 car bought five years ago, and since totaled in a highway accident, is still worth $10,000. The actual monetary value of the great luxury liner is undoubtedly on the negative side of a cash flow chart: reduced by the high cost of salvage.

Likewise, rumors persist that untold riches lie waiting to be recovered from within the confines of her dark, forbidding hull: paintings, cargo, money and jewelry in the various safes, and valuables left in staterooms by passengers in their haste to escape. Peter Gimbel brought up one safe and, despite its load of cash, proved that salvage alone for its own rewards could never pay for the expenditures involved. Cargo that once had value is worthless today, after more than three decades of salt water immersion. Paintings and murals have long since ceased to exist. In short, a commercial venture is doomed to failure as an economic investment.

If simply seeing and experiencing the Grand Dame of the Sea is not compensation enough, she does offer remuneration in the form of souvenirs, or artifacts, to those willing to exert their energies to exploring her many decks and picking through piles of unrecognizable rubbish for baubles of historic or intrinsic interest.

I have searched through the remains of many cabins, painstakingly poking through the debris for these personal treasures. Some dives have been incredibly fulfilling, others have been merely fun; none were disappointing. Exploration for its own sake is the best reward. If during my brief sojourns along her hallowed corridors I found a relic of the past, it was a premium accepted with pleasure.

Once I swam over an enclosure I had seen year after year. On this particular occasion the upper facade had rusted away to reveal a cabinet full of cut glassware: crystal goblets, brandy snifters, long stemmed cocktail glasses, tumblers, water and wine glasses. Among them were French onion soup bowls and lids. This newfound bonanza was soon depleted by a host of divers seeking the same thing I was: a memento of this most famous of all diveable shipwrecks.

On a quite different tour I entered the First Class Cocktail Lounge, hoping to find stacks of liquor bottles and wine decanters. The bar stools stood like silent sentinels, protruding horizontally from the tilted deck, but the serving counter was gone: broken free of its mounts and smashed into a

pile of rubble at the bottom of the hull. I was sorely disappointed. I kept going, swimming along the portside corridor past a glass topped cocktail table still bolted to the deck. Just beyond, in the dull brown field of debris, I saw the rim of a demitasse saucer pinned under a flat, rectangular block. I yanked the obstruction out of the way and tossed it aside, flipping it over in the process to see if anything was stuck to its bottom.

The block turned out to be a ceramic panel, one of the few works of art that had survived the ravages of the sea. The artist was Romano Rui. Each panel was an independant scene which rolled over into the topic of the two adjacent panels, the whole depicting a sequence of people and animals and ancient devices from preindustrial times. Continued digging exposed more of these panels, my most cherished treasures from the *Andrea Doria*.

Courtesy of the Italian Line.

Still I comb the quiet corridors, delve into the most intimate corners of the wreck. Always I have the thought of finding memorabilia embossed with the shipping line crest, "Italia," for those demonstrate best that those items once resided on a ship of the Italian Line. Thus it was that after many years and numerous dives on the *Andrea Doria*, I located a spot on the deck plans that offered the highest potential for these and other priceless artifacts.

A small room in the First Class Foyer was listed as "negozio." Translated in the legend as "gift shop," this was the ship's store that sold high priced souvenirs to wealthy first class passengers. It was centrally located to catch the eye of travelers as they were embarking on their long ocean voyages, or were loitering as the ship was warped into port.

According to the deck plans, reaching the gift shop seemed deceptively easy. The entrance point was the same hole that Gimbel had cut through the hull to recover the safe, and through which I had already gone to reach the china in the dining room. It was a straight drop down to the centerline of the ship. I studied the plans of the entire area in order to familiarize myself with other rooms and bulkheads I might encounter.

The only problem that developed was that, because of the depth, and because the dining room was still yielding its riches, no one was willing to help me in my quest. The certainty of recovering china dissuaded others from chasing romance. This enterprise was my own.

When I rolled over the rail of the *Sea Hunter*, it was with the trepidation I feel before every deep dive. I had no intention of charging into the wreck in a bullish frame of mind. Visibility on the hull was ten to fifteen feet, with great streamers of plankton that reminded me of a bowl of egg drop soup. On the previous dive I had shackled the anchor line to a Promenade Deck stanchion only ten feet from the Foyer opening.

I let go the twisted nylon twenty feet above the plated hull, and dropped straight down through the massive hole. It was dark inside, like the lining of a pocket; I checked my spare light as I descended. In order to orient myself, I faced aft: in the direction of the gift shop. I dragged my right hand across the linoleum covered deck as a way of maintaining some touch with reality in this great, Stygian mausoleum.

To my left, the drop ceiling hung loosely on rusting wires. Acoustical tiles had long since vanished, and pipes and electrical cables bulged through the latticework. A bulkhead appeared in front of me, laden with debris that had rained down from collapsed partitions. The corridor was supported by a ventilator shaft and the upper side of the gift shop. When I looked up, the comforting green glow of light from the doorway was thirty feet overhead. I slid deeper into the wreck.

My powerful white beam was swallowed up by the blackness, penetrating not more than five or ten feet despite the inner clarity: the plankton did not float inside. Tiny swirls of silt eddied off the linoleum from the touch of my speeding fingers: I was sinking too fast. I touched the inflator

These ceramic panels are the work of Italian artist Romano Rui. The panel on the left shows a repair that was made prior to the sinking. The panel on the right still retains the thin veneer of marine growth.

The glass doors are the Gift Shop front. To the right is the corridor that leads to the Dining Room. Courtesy of the Italian Line.

button on my suit, let in a blast of cold air. The added buoyancy slowed my descent. I hoisted my gauge panel in front of my eyes. I still had plenty of air as I passed the 220 foot mark. The gift shop should be right in front of me.

My light picked out a rust covered barrier, indistinct. It was not solid, but I could not see through it. I was still drifting downward. Then the barrier ended, and I moved under it. I should not have to swim more than ten feet before encountering the back wall of the gift shop. When I estimated my forward progress as fifteen feet, I stopped. My heart was pounding. My dive light, an extension of my hand, stabbed into the darkness and touched nothing. I glanced at my depth gauge: 230 feet.

I was too deep, and too far in. What I saw did not fit with what I expected to find. It was time to call it quits, to go back to the drawing board, to correlate my visual references with the deck plans, to try to reason out why the gift shop was not where I thought it should be.

I rose slightly and backed out. The light above me was blocked by the barrier I had ducked under. My exhaust bubbles cascaded against a bulkhead just over my head. I reached up and touched it, walking my fingers over the orange, rusty, metallic surface.

When it ended, I put more air into my suit, kicked gently with my fins. Still, I could see no light above me. I hugged the floor, more for stability than orientation. I kept a vertical attitude as I rose, searching aloft with my light. I ascended some ten feet. In front of me was a protruding shelf covered with deep mud. Half buried under the brown silt lay a porcelain figurine with cupped hands.

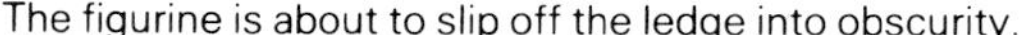
The figurine is about to slip off the ledge into obscurity.

I centered my camera, and fingered the shutter release. The strobe burned the image onto the film. Slowly, I panned the shelf and took a series of pictures before any itinerant swirls of silt obscured the view. Then I let go the camera, felt the reassuring tug on the wrist lanyard, and opened my goodie bag. I eased the ceramic object out of the mud and shook it clean: it was a caroling angel, reading from an open music book. Nearby I found two cherubs, with colored wings, trailing slender electrical wires that were connected to a tiny light bulb.

Nothing else was immediately obvious, so I placed the art objects in the mesh bag and kicked my way up. I was still enveloped in the murk when I ran into an overhanging bulkhead. Slowly I spun around until my back was toward the shelf. In front of me hung a shroud of thick cables: during my descent they had hidden the gift shop like a bamboo curtain. I had passed underneath them, like diving into a pool and coming up behind a waterfall. Now, by keeping close to the vertical deck, I pushed them out of the way and moved toward the middle of the Foyer.

The oblong glow of light that was the opening in the hull was a welcome sight. Once clear of the wires I charged upward. In a moment I was outside the wreck. During decompression I kept staring through the mesh at the hand painted pastels of the figurines.

On the *Sea Hunter*, my jubilation was shared with my fellow divers. I wasted no time in pulling out the deck plans while the imagery of the dive was still fresh in my mind. When I plotted depths and distances I realized that at the 230 foot level I had entered the corridor below the gift shop.

The figurines on the deck of the boat.

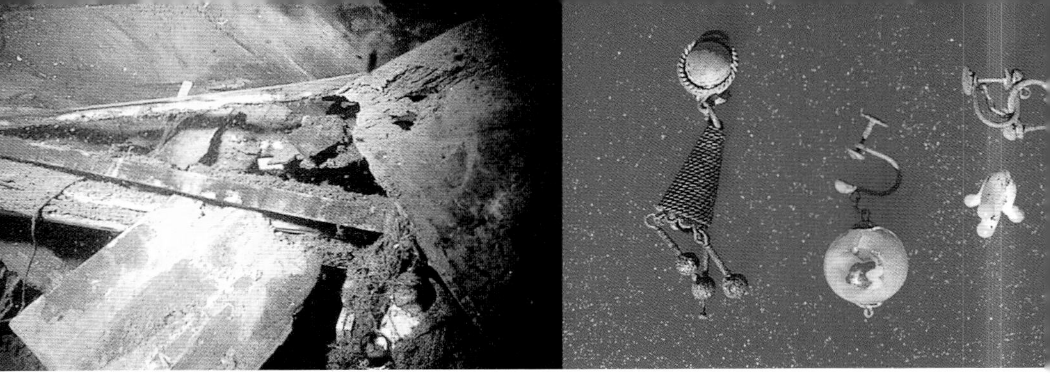

Visible among the boards of the collapsed storage cabinet (left) are earrings shown on the right.

Now that I knew the layout, I could quickly return to the right spot and look for more souvenir items. But the cables had to be avoided: they could easily entangle a diver's tanks or hoses, and might be difficult to cut with a divers knife.

Elated as I was over my finds, I did not have the opportunity to revisit the gift shop. A severe squall hammered the *Sea Hunter* until it rolled and pitched with a twisting, sickening motion. The Coast Guard warned that the worst was yet to come. Sal reluctantly made the decision to pull anchor and head for home. The trip was over.

However, two weeks later found me retracing my path to the *Andrea Doria*, this time courtesy of Captain Steve Bielenda and the *Wahoo*. With the dining room still a hot spot, and an attraction for divers, Steve's plans for tying in by the Foyer opening coincided with my own. Steve grappled the wreck, and John Lachenmeyer and I swam down with another line that we were to shackle to the Promenade Deck stanchion. We ran into trouble right away.

The grapnel had scraped along the hull until it swept over the edge of the superstructure, where it dropped deep and snagged in a trawler net's lead line. From a depth of 190 feet I could see the bow windlass of the *Andrea Doria*: more than a hundred feet from where we wanted to be. The current was so strong that I could not swim against it carrying the chain and shackle, even though John was taking the strain off the two hundred odd feet of rope. Worse yet, the *Wahoo* pulled so hard on the grapnel that we could not get enough slack to free it. We had to cut the net apart to free the grapnel, and abort the tie in. We had to wait in frustration for sufficient surface interval to elapse before we could safely make a repetitive dive.

Steve regrappled the wreck, and this time Janet Bieser went down to tie in. The situation was similar, except that the grapnel was closer to the hull. She was able to effect the tie in. But for me, and for those who wanted to look for china, the position was all wrong. The line was tied in too far forward. When I went down next, although I was able to swim to the Foyer opening and drop inside, I did not feel I had enough safety margin to undertake further exploration of the gift shop. I wanted to have an anchor

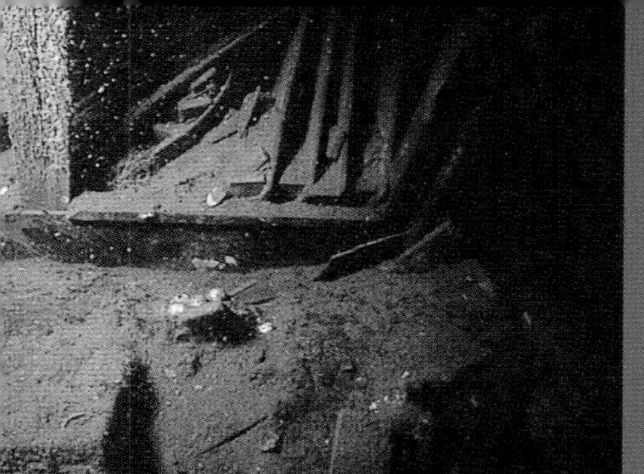

The slats are storage drawers now on a vertical axis. The jewelry they contained slid to the bottom, or spilled out onto the mud-filled shelf. The badly eroded bracelet visible in the center foreground of the left picture is shown (right) after it was restored.

line right outside the hole so the ascent from the Foyer could be made immediately, without having to make a swim along the gargantuan hull that would use up so much air. It was a safety factor I was not willing to concede.

Craig Steinmetz relieved me of this predicament. He took down a third line, swam it all the way to the proper stanchion, and tied it in. Now, at last, I felt confident in making another excursion into the cable covered gift shop. This time, I knew right where I was going.

I took particular notice of the wires hanging in front of the shelf. They were not as thick as I remembered, or imagined. During my previous examination, with a casual glance borne of the unfamiliar, the thick encrustration disguised their true nature. Now, I studied them in detail. Since they were falling out of the ceiling, to my left, it was better to pass them adjacent to the vertical floor. I hugged the linoleum, slipped through the spider web, and in a moment found myself inside a cage.

I shot a series of photographs, this time catching the back wall consisting of long upright pieces of wood I took to be the ends of drawers, now stacked horizontally. Their contents must have spilled out onto the shelf. When I looked carefully I noticed tiny spots of color in the mud: jewels that were adorning bracelets and earrings.

Delicately, I plucked out whatever I could see. As soon as I touched anything on the narrow shelf, the silt churned up and threw a pall over the pile of smothered debris. At the end of ten minutes, at a depth of 220 feet, I had precious little to show for my efforts: a ring, a badly eroded bracelet, a couple of earrings, and some beads. The trip ended without any significant finds.

Undiscouraged by my lack of success, instead of pondering my disappointment, I spent the winter studying my photographs. They showed precious little except a deep pile of muck that clung to a two foot wide ledge. I reasoned that if any souvenir items had fallen out of the drawers onto the shelf, they should still be there: but buried under the claylike mud. I proposed a new plan of attack. The next year I hit pay dirt on the first dive.

I opened my mesh bag, plunged my hand deep into the muck, and like an amusement park ten-cent grab claw scooped out great handfuls of mud, and deposited the clumps in the bag. Visibility was reduced to zero after the first earth movement, so I had no idea what, if anything, I was putting into the goody bag. I could barely make out red and green dots, glints of brass and silver. I felt like a game show contestant who was given a shopping cart and ten minutes in which to fill it with whatever he could lay his hands on.

Since there was nothing to stand or lean on, I had to keep kicking in order to maintain elevation as the bag became heavier. I also had to make sure that my movements did not shove me back into the mass of cables behind me. Despite my eagerness, and in keeping with good diving practice, I left the gift shop when only half my prescribed bottom time had passed. Greed can be an ugly beast. I always allowed for the unexpected.

Enveloped as I was in a thick cloud of black ooze, I was no longer able to see the gift shop shelf. I relied for orientation on the blue linoleum barely visible in the suffused light. As I started backing out, I felt cables scraping over my tanks. My pulse rate doubled as I froze, tried to maintain my depth by gripping a loose board, and slowly pulled myself forward. I entertained a sharp mental picture of those cables wrapping around my tank valves or regulator first stages, or catching on my decompression reel.

When I sensed no more contact, I executed an agonizingly slow about face. I saw nothing but a fog of brown particles. I pushed my way along the

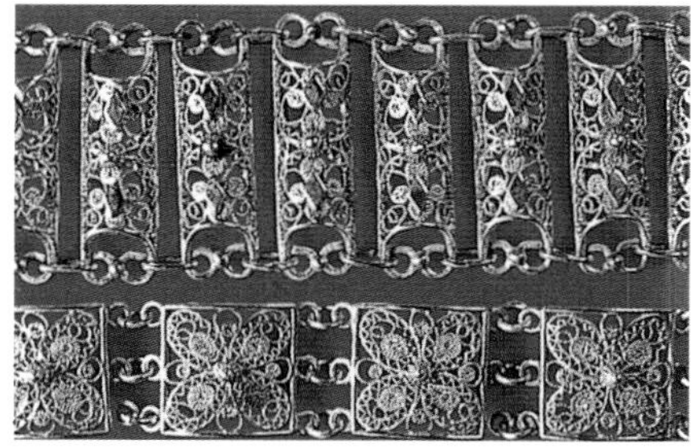

floor, trying to outdistance the stirred up silt before making my ascent, so as not to encounter the cables that were undoubtedly reaching out for me. When I finally broke into the clear I saw that the floor pattern had changed. A series of vertical shelves lay before me, one on top of the other, forcing me away from where I should be going. I followed these until I came to a blank wall that should not have been there.

Again I froze, and tried to reason out the dilemma of disorientation. I was free of the mud, so in ample visibility I could study the area. The shelves had a curious tread design on one side, a rounded lip, and bare wood on the other. After many seconds of pondering, I realized that these were risers, and that I had overshot my mark by crossing the breadth of the Foyer Lounge, and ascended the stairwell half way up to the next deck. The Main Deck had no exit to the outer hull. Without turning, I backtracked, all the time looking overhead. Soon I saw that comforting green glow. In one fluid motion I ascended through the opening and up the anchor line. When I checked my pressure gauge and watch I saw that I still had plenty of air for decompression, and was one minute under my planned bottom time. I began to control my breathing while I made a long, slow, controlled ascent.

As I settled down at the fifty foot stop, I glanced through the mesh of the goody bag. Clumps of mud were breaking up as I was jostled by the jerking anchor line Objects began to appear: paired earrings, pendants, medallions, broaches, bracelets, charms, rings, and beads. Unbelievably, a

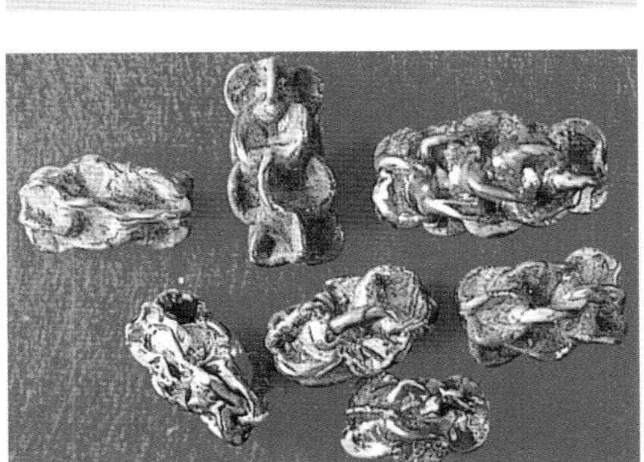

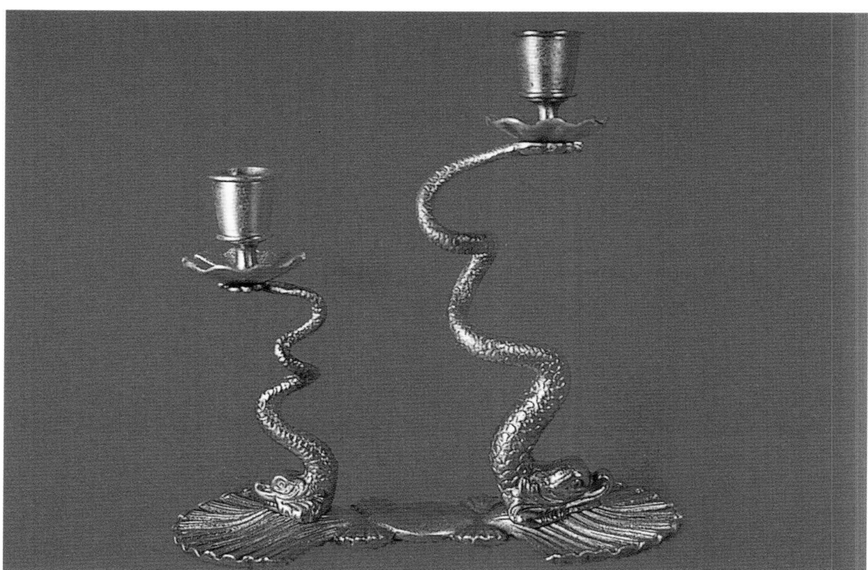

large brass candelabra in the form of two stylized sea serpents, with teeth and scales, lay right on top. I never did understand how I could have picked it up without feeling its size or shape.

Also in the bag were brass statuettes, porcelain figurines, a silver statue of winged Mercury carrying the caduceus and standing in the mouth of Jupiter. Ashtrays with salutations or the names of prominent Italian cities were signed on the back by the artist. Rosary cases still contained rosaries and Christ on the cross.

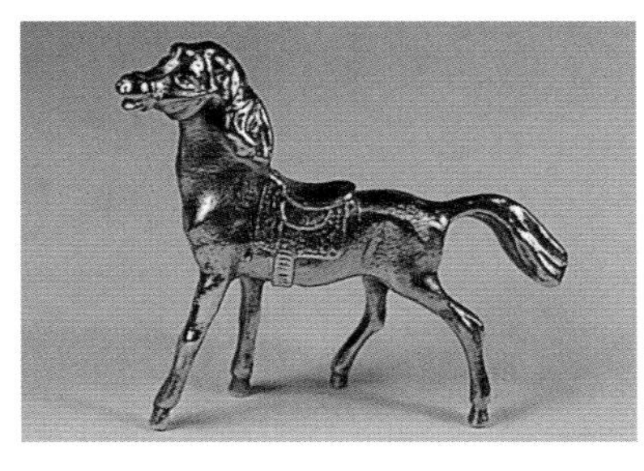

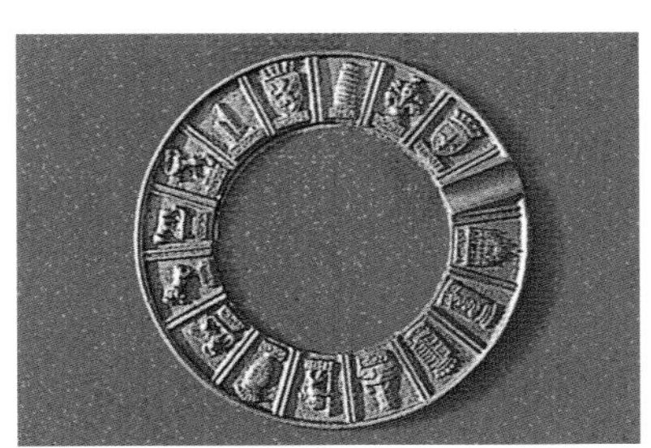

PACE
A-CHI-ENTRA
SALUTE
A-CHI-ESCE

The spoon shows clearly in the center of the picture.

I saw nothing imprinted with the much desired "Italia," but I went one better. My heart skipped a beat as I grabbed through the mesh with mitted hands, fondled the handle of a child-sized silver spoon, and spun it around so I could see into the bowl. There was a painting of the ship, and the words "Andrea Doria."

The *Wahoo* went wild with rejoicing as I sifted through the mud and disclosed my finds. For safe keeping, I deposited the jewelry through the neck of a plastic milk bottle. The one gallon jug was nearly full by the time I was done. There were no duplicates, for each piece of jewelry was individually hand crafted in Italy: no chance of a woman passenger meeting another wearing the same pair of earrings.

For me, the *Andrea Doria* has yielded her treasures: not just in the value of what I have recovered, not just in the photographs of her remains, but in the knowledge that, had I not reclaimed these precious relics from their precarious ledge, they would have been lost forever in the collapsing hull, torn and broken apart by rending iron beams, buried beyond reach, and dissolved by Nature's relentless chemical action.

To a collector, these artifacts are invaluable; to me, they are priceless. They are more than mere ornaments, more than trinkets, more than yesteryear's art. They are the culture of an era. They do not represent only the majesty of the Grand Dame of the Sea, they are rare examples of the luxury, the charisma, and the mystique of a time when ocean liners plied the broad reaches of the Atlantic and transported rich and poor alike between the Old World and the New.

These artifacts are history, and man's quest for history never ends.

The gift shop also carried souvenir spoons depicting other ships of the Italian Line: the names were different, but the painting was the same. Steve Bielenda preserved the tablet pages by chemical treatment and freezing.

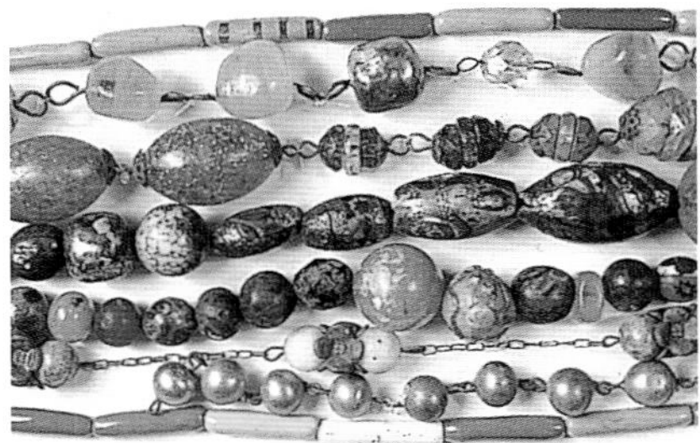

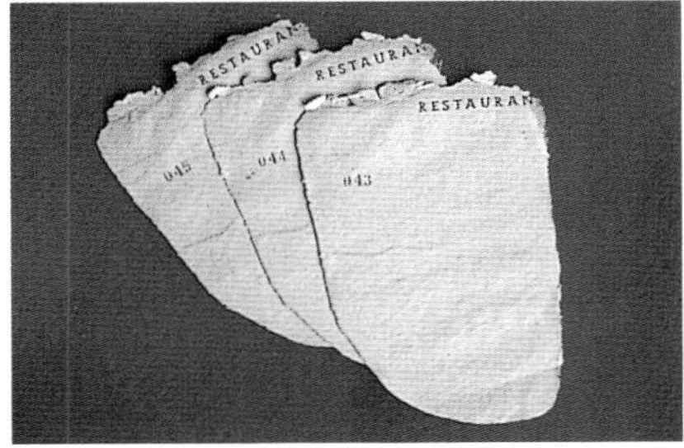

The wooden block protruding from the mud (above) is a manger (right) with the Madonna and child. Below: Steve Bielenda sticks his hand into the gift shop mud.

CHAPTER 6
THE SWEET CHIME OF SUCCESS

"The difficult we do immediately. The impossible may take a bit longer."

—Rear Admiral Ben Moreel (of the Seabees)

Photo by Tom Brown.

Above: Photo by Charles J. Humphries.

Below: Courtesy of The Mariners Museum, Newport News, VA.

The Sweet Chime of Success

One of man's greatest attributes is his willingness to work together. Even as an individual he is Nature's most formidable foe, combining intelligence, stealth, and sheer will power in a way that makes him a superior adversary, capable of accomplishing great deeds. As a group, a tribe, a nation, he has caused the march of a civilization that has led him to world dominance. Working with many heads, and many hands, he has achieved greatness.

Team work is a force to be reckoned with. This is a tale of team work.

Bill Nagle's first recollection of television, as a four year old toddler, was of his parents sitting him in front of an ancient black and white set to watch a great sea catastrophe, the sinking of the *Andrea Doria*. Bill vividly remembers adolescent years viewing the adventures of Sea Hunt. When he took his diving course at the tender age of sixteen, his mind was already filled with images of adventures underwater. But more than a decade would pass before he gained the experience to dive on that wreck which he had seen at so impressionable an age.

His one main goal was to descry that famous ship with his own eyes, to touch her with his own hands. In due time, he did. But once he started exploring the Grand Dame of the Sea, he found that he needed more. Throughout the years of annual charters to the wreck site he studied her still gracefull hull, probed her burgeoning entrances, collected mementoes of his visits—and dreamed. In the back of his mind was an idea. . . .

During my many years of diving with Bill we shared numerous ventures, experiences, and notions. We worked together on udnerwater projects, collected relics, organized dives, did research, bought ships' plans and photographs: each with our pet aims. One of Bill's fantasies was to recover the *Andrea Doria's* bell: the ultimate artifact from the ultimate wreck. The project was within reason, but could not be done alone. For many years we discussed it, each time outlining in more detail what the expedition would require.

We needed a practiced dive team, a serviceable charter boat, and time.

Only a few divers had the required experience, the time available, and the willingness to go. Only those who had already dived the *Andrea Doria* could be considered: this was not the time to learn the wreck. Bill contacted friends and fellow divers, and asked them to volunteer their services for the endeavor. Gradually, a team of seven evolved.

Chartering a boat proved more difficult. We had no way of knowing how long the job would take, how cooperative the weather would be, or what contingencies might occur. Charter boats operate on a strict timeable, bound fore and aft by other charters. We needed an open ended arrangement containing some latitude in scheduling. After several deals fell through, Bill took the bull by the horns: he bought his own dive boat and went into the charter business.

After years of restless planning, the bell project was about to become a reality. The only thing left was to set a date.

When we loaded the thousands of pounds of tanks, dive gear, ice, and food, onto the *Seeker* on a hot Fourth of July, the biggest question in my mind—and my greatest fear—was not if we had the capability of recovering the bronze bell, but—was it there?

In all my research into the many salvage and photographic expeditions to the *Andrea Doria* I had never come across any reference to the ship's bell. Salvors had different objectives, photographers had different subjects. Yet, in more than one museum picture of the ship, the bell shows prominently on the bow, just forward of the spare anchor. When underwater film makers were busily cleaning off the bronze letters on the port hull, and taking pictures of the name, they were only twenty feet away from the bell davit—and none had bothered to look for it.

With this thought in mind, my anticipation was mixed with anxiety as I jumped into unsettled seas after our late afternoon arrival at the wreck site. With a marker buoy placed at the tip of the wreck's bow, the grapnel had been dropped approximately seventy feet aft of the stem. The first job was to locate the hawser opening adjacent to the breakwater, and to secure a permanent down line that would not pull free as the boat swung in an endless arc according to the vagaries of North Atlantic current.

My dive buddy was Tom Packer, a sheet metal worker from West Berlin, New Jersey, who was recently married, and was sweating out his wife's first pregnancy. Kim was due to deliver in a couple weeks. Just before leaving for the bell project, Tom rushed her to the obstetrician with false labor pains. The doctor understood her nervousness, told her not to worry, and sent her home. Still, Tom was understandably concerned. During the long day of boat preparation at the Brielle dock, he poured quarters into the public phone as if it were a slot machine that refused to pay off. He called her again from Block Island when we pulled in for fuel. But once in the water, his concentration on the task at hand put all other thoughts out of mind.

In order to operate most efficiently, Tom dragged the heavy tie-in rope down the anchor line while I shot ahead to locate the specific hawser opening, third aft from the bow. The water grew cold and darksome as I descended. No wreck appeared until I reached a depth of 200 feet; as my eyes adjusted to the dim light I made out a vague silhouette in the gloom before me. With the hull lying approximately north-south, and with the superstructure facing east, the westering sun cast the upperworks of the wreck in shadow.

As I got closer I was able to distinguish shapes: windlasses, winch drums, and the spare anchor still secured to the deck. This was the exact spot we wanted. I swam up to the high side of the wreck and found the hawser opening right where it was supposed to be. Two mooring bitts lay under it, just as shown on the ship's plans. I noticed a current above the hull that had been blocked by the bulk of the wreck. I returned to the grapnel happy that our task would be so easy.

I did not reckon on the aciton of the sea. The heaving boat was working the anchor line up and down. The grapnel had fallen free; only the chain draped over a metal projection prevented the boat from drifting off. Tom was only twenty feet away, clearly visible, pulling the mooring line by the shackle. I jammed my hand against the chain, hoping to hold it in place until Tom reached the wreck. But surface conditions were too rough; the surge ripped the line out of its precarious hold.

The grapnel caught the hose of my pressure gauge, whipped me around and upside down, and dragged me through the water like a lassoed heifer. As I struggled to extricate myself I could see Tom in one direction, the colossal hull in the other. Already the wreck was receding, an indiscriminate gray shape in the distance. Despite the buoyancy of my drysuit, the weight of the grapnel was taking me deeper.

With nighttime on the way this was a crucial tie-in. If we had to drop a sand anchor overnight and send down another team in the morning, it could mean the loss of a full day in our mission. We had determined that, due to the extreme working depth at which we expected to operate, each diver would make only one dive daily.

When I finally disentangled myself I made a snap judgement. The current was negligible in the lee of the hull, now almost invisible. I threw away the grapnel and struck out for the wreck. I kicked as hard as I could. The machinery came back into view, looming above me. I reached a protruding winch drum and stopped to regain my breath. Tom was nowhere to be seen; I was on my own.

My first priority now was to establish a combination decompression line and marker buoy. I swam up to the port gunwale, passed over the encrusted two foot tall letters that spelled out the ship's name, and hooked my leg through the hawser opening that was to be the permanent mooring spot. The current over the top of the wreck was strong, but not unreasonable. I removed my emergency decompression reel from its position on the back of my tanks; 350 feet of closely wound sisal rope lay neatly on the wooden spool. I tied an orange liftbag to the end of the line, inflated the bag, and held onto the ends of the dowel as the rope unreeled and the liftbag screamed for the surface.

The waves on the surface yanked hard on the reel, making it difficult to tie the line to the wreck. As soon as I spooled a leader off the reel, the slack was dragged away from me. Finally, I jammed the entire reel through the hawser opening, let it fall, then dropped down, grabbed it, and circled it around the upright rope. I made a gigantic knot, then cut the rope from the reel.

I still had plenty of air and bottom time, so I went off to look for the bell davit. I dropped along the breakwater to the spare anchor, at the center line of the ship: the depth was 210 feet. Then I moved forward until I saw a goosenecked davit sticking out horizontally. It was empty.

I scraped the encrustation off the end, exposing two tiny ears and a thick drift pin. Nothing was broken; it just seemed as if the bell had been removed and the pin replaced. Disappointed, I swam back to the upper hull, returned to my sisal line, and made a slow ascent. I had been down fifteen minutes, so a thirty minute decompression was required.

Due to the current, the line did not rise straight up, but angled toward the surface like a kite in the wind. At forty feet I had to hold on hard. Above my head, I saw that the liftbag had been pulled underwater by the tremendous drag on the two hundred feet of sisal. It was not until I reached the ten foot stage, where the bag was floating, that I could add more air to it and force it to break the surface. The waves still passed over the liftbag, but this was an advantage in that I did not suffer the jerking, armwrenching motion of an anchor line decompression. When my decompression was completed, I rose into the froth of choppy seas.

The *Seeker* was nowhere in sight.

I struggled to the top of the crests for a look down current, but the horizon showed only green swells and fading blue sky. The ocean was as barren in all other directions. I felt helplessly, frighteningly alone.

Despite my anxiety, I forced myself to lie as quietly as I could in the bouncing waves. Rather than tire myself out looking constantly for the boat, I put my face in the water and held onto the line. Every few minutes I popped up to scan the whitecaps for any sign of my friends. I could not even see the white bleach bottle that was the marker buoy.

I began entertaining some very bad thoughts. Knowing that the boat was adrift, I wondered if the anchor line was wrapped around the propeller. Perhaps the engine would not start. Maybe the battery went dead. Possibly the electrical system had shorted out. A leak in the fiberglas hull may have flooded the air intakes. As the sun got lower in the sky I realized that I might have to spend the night on the float.

I switched to my snorkel in order to save air for inflating my suit, and the bobbing liftbag. I was growing weaker; the accidental swallowing of salt water and the three to four foot waves were making me seasick. It was vitally important that I remain on the wreck site; if I drifted off I would be nothing more than an insignificant dot in the vast Atlantic Ocean, at the whim of shifting tides and currents. After an hour of loneliness, I rigged a line to the liftbag and tied it to my tank harness; now I could rest my arms.

Finally, gloriously, as I topped the crest of a wave, I saw a white speck in the distance. The thirty-five foot Maine Coaster drew near on a sheering course. I saw an arm thrust out suddenly in my direction. In a trice the *Seeker's* lurching bow turned my way. Bill maneuvered alongside and idled the engine. John Moyer lowered the ladder into the water. I hate boats, and always have; but I was never so happy to be on one as I was at that moment.

Tom threw his arms around me. "Man, we all thought you were gone."

As the gang surrounded me and helped me doff my gear, the story came out in bits and pieces. Tom had been dragged deep by the sinking grapnel like the weight at the end of a pendulum. His last glimpse of me was floating down into the depths with no wreck in sight. He let go the shackle and down line, and climbed up the anchor rope. Despite the short time down, he still had to decompress. When he broke the surface he reported me missing.

Those on board did not believe him at first, and forced him back down to extend his decompression. They thought he had come straight up after a long dive, when in reality he had made a short dive and adequate decompression. They dealt with Tom as a patient who should not be allowed to prescribe his own treatment. They figured he might be showing residual narcosis.

Reinforcing their beliefs in Tom's misinformation was the bleach bottle that still floated idly off the bow of the *Seeker*. They figured I must have managed to resnag the grapnel and tie it in. In fact, the grapnel caught the buoy line and dragged it along as the boat drifted in the current. Since my liftbag had been pulled quickly underwater by the drag on the line, they never saw it. When they finally let Tom on the boat, and realized that I was not with him, they assumed the worst.

John Moyer was supposed to be part of the dive team, but two weeks previously he suffered a severe case of the bends following a deep dive in the Mud Hole. He had to be evacuated to a recompression chamber by Coast Guard helicopter. His symptoms of paralysis were relieved during treatment, but the doctor warned him against diving again for at least a month. John came on the trip anyway, his captain's license and boat handling experience a valuable asset to the trip. During a check of the navigational electronics, he noticed that the *Seeker's* present loran position placed them more than half a mile from the wreck. The crew pulled in the lines, and Bill steered the boat back through the waves to the proper coordinates. Only because I maintained position had they found me awaiting anxiously their return.

It was a contest as to whether I was more happy to see them, or they to see me. Personally, I think I won.

The news I brought was unwanted. Our hopes of finding the bell sitting placidly in its davit were dashed. This meant instituting a programmed search pattern, either on the lower part of the hull where it may have fallen, or in the sand. But the first job at hand was to get a permanent mooring line shackled into the hull. With darkness not too far off, the next dive team hastened to get dressed.

Mike Boring, a computer technician and diving instructor (yes, some of them can dive, too) residing in Laurel, Maryland, had once been a commercial oyster diver in the Chesapeake Bay. For several years while attending night school, he collected the delicious and marketable shellfish in all kinds of conditions, including going under the ice when the bay froze over in the winter. He had thousands of hours underwater, more than the rest of us put together.

Kenny Gascon, a transmission repair shop owner who had recently sold out and bought into a dive shop business, lived near Mike, in Oxon Hill, Maryland. He had been one of Mike's students, one of the few who had stayed with the sport over the years. Now they were friends as well as diving buddies.

Artie Kirchner, better known as Big Artie (six foot six, and two hundred sixty pounds after a shave and a haircut) had taken a week off from his electrical contracting business to be here. Already he had jobs waiting for his return, and a restaurant that was nearing its opening date. Because of such pressing engagements, he wanted to get the bell, get it fast, and get back to Dover, New Jersey. Although we planned to dive in two man teams, he decided to go along with Mike and Kenny because there was not enough time before sunset for him and Bill to make their dive. At no time would a dive team enter the water until the previous team had completed decompression. That was one of the safety concessions we had made.

Bill ran the boat past my liftbag and the three jumped overboard.

Above: The bow watch keeps an eye on decompressing divers. Below: Kenny Gascon, Mike Boring, and Art Kirchner made the all-important permanent tie-in.

Artie did the bull work of carrying the chain and shackle down my decompression line. Working together, the trio dropped the chain through the *Andrea Doria's* forward hawser hole and made fast the bolt. They also had time to do some scouting. It was dark by the time they got back on the boat. Their report on the empty davit confirmed our worst fears.

That night we made plans for the search.

The morning of our second day over the wreck was rough—but not rough enough to halt diving operations. Mike and Kenny were the first team to hit the water. During their twenty minute dive they made sure the mooring shackle was still secure, attached a line from there to the heavily encrusted davit, then lowered it as a guideline into the darkness below.

This paved the way for Tom and me. Due to the choppy seas, not much light penetrated to the hull. It became even darker as we dropped to the davit at 210 feet. We both checked our gauges and, as planned, made sure we felt confident enough to continue our descent. The water temperature was 49°, the visibility a dark fifteen feet. We exchanged okay signs.

I took my hand off the davit and let air out of my drysuit. Slowly, I dropped into the black abyss. Facing the deck, I swung my light back and forth, hoping to find that the bell had fallen and snagged on the machinery. Tom's light shone down from a few feet above. I kept a constant check on my gauges: air, depth, and time. The digital readout passed 220 feet, then 230. It was gloomy down there. The remains of trawler nets posed a constant threat.

Above: Tom Packer checks the shackle pin, as each team did on every dive. Below: Tom pauses by the davit before we continue our descent to the sand.

At 235 feet the wreck ended abruptly, as did the weighted down line, but the sand was nowhere in sight. Since we were only fifty feet from the bow, the hull was curving toward the centerline of the ship. At this point the wreck did not touch bottom.

I glanced along the starboard rail; it was a good place for the bell to have caught if it had fallen from its perch. This entire section of the hull was crushed and bent. Since the ship had sunk bow first, the weight of the hull had twisted the forward section out of shape. After a moment I shook my head at Tom, and continued the descent. I felt a pounding in my head: the slightly numbing effect of nitrogen narcosis. I shrugged it off. I plopped down on the sand and stared at my gauges. The digital readout was easy to interpret: 248 feet.

Tom alighted next to me. Sand swirled up around him as he gave me the okay sign. I nodded, and showed him the gauge. When I looked up, I could see no sign of the immense hull of the *Andrea Doria*. Even my powerful light could not cut through the particulate matter. The slender cone of light did not reach far, and outside its beam was total blackness.

Around us was nothing but white sand, and a few small pieces of wreckage. We moved slowly, not wanting to get too far from where we had come down, but needing to scout along the axis of the ship. I saw a familiar red form in front of me. Years of wreck diving habits took effect. Instinctively, I reached out and grabbed the two pound lobster, and put it in my goody bag. I heard Tom cheering, laughing, and shouting through his regulator. He pointed to the steel shelter out of which he had just spooked the lobster.

We ranged along under the edge of the wreck, searching with our lights for something bell-like protruding from the sand. I kept one hand on my gauge panel, monitoring constantly my air and bottom time. It did not take long before we accepted the fact that if the bell had fallen from its davit, it was long since buried.

We returned to the tracks in the sand made by our landing, and rose vertically. I felt security and a warm glow of safety when I saw the ghostly railing appear overhead. I placed my hand on it for stability. Now we followed the rail aft: the bell may have fallen and rolled down the incline. But when we reached the breakwater, a partition running from port to starboard across the ship, we knew that it was nowhere around. We came straight up, over the huge spare anchor positioned amidships, and right to the anchor line. Our total time on the bottom had been twelve minutes, but it had felt like a lifetime. After decompressing, we reported our findings.

Bill and Artie went down next. They searched along the deck and machinery spaces, and retraced the route along the starboard rail: even the most experienced diver can overlook an object when it is covered with and distorted by marine growth, or enshrouded by rotting trawler nets. They found nothing.

The next morning a strong current swept across the wreck. The hand-over-hand pull down the anchor line was difficult, but on the wreck itself the hull deflected the speeding water and created a pillow effect. When Mike and Kenny attempted to conduct another sand search, the current almost sucked them under the wreck. As Mike lowered himself below the edge, still clinging to the railing, his legs were swept back in the strong tide. They had to claw their way back to safety. Anyone dropping off to the sand would have been carried away, forced to make an ascent far from the security of the anchor line.

The only good thing about the next two days was the weather. The ocean was as calm as an inland lake. The sun set magnificently in a crystal blue sky. We took turns on radar watch at night, so we would not get run down by passing freighters and tankers. The stars shone with a brilliance not otherwise visible—or appreciable—when surrounded by the glaring lights of cities and civilization. Meteors flashed swiftly but silently across the heavens. The lights of fishing trawlers bobbed all around as their hardy crews worked throughout the night.

For a while a fog rolled in, obscuring all but the few feet of deck space pierced by the cabin searchlight. Before she sank, *Andrea Doria* drifted into the separation zone between the northerly inbound lane and the southerly outbound lane. According to suggested rules of the road, ship traffic should not pass over the wreck site. Daylight observation disproved this theory. I was understandably concerned when the radar screen showed a blip a scant half mile away. I watched it breathlessly, ready to sever the anchor line and to crank over the diesel engine. A supertanker could run

DV

down this thirty-five foot boat and never feel it. As I scanned the misty horizon, the unknown vessel slipped by without ever sounding its fog horn.

It was under exactly such conditions that the *Stockholm*, traveling east on a clear night, rammed the *Andrea Doria* coming out of a pea-soup fog. In the area of the Nantucket Shoals, the fog could come and go within minutes, and the fog banks often ended with a sharp line of demarkation.

During the day, between dives, and to the accompaniment of the double sonic booms from the French Concorde, we fished. Cod and pollock were plentiful, growing to five feet in length and weighing up to forty pounds. This epicurian bonanza made the *Andrea Doria* a favorite fishing spot for the head boats from Montauk. We quickly learned to put but a single hook on the line; hauling two monster fish from the depths was too much of a workout. The cod were a welcome addition to our diet of canned and frozen food.

Blue sharks swam by majestically, attracted by the blood of gutted fish. These elasmobranchs, relatives of the fish characterized by a cartilaginous skeleton, possess a notoriety that is not borne out by direct contact: they did not bother us in the water. John Moyer used a cod head for bait and, after a forty-five minute struggle, landed a ten-and- a-half foot specimen. He spent many hours slicing out meat and whittling the jaw down to a mantelpiece curio full of sharp pointed teeth. The blue shark is edible, as well.

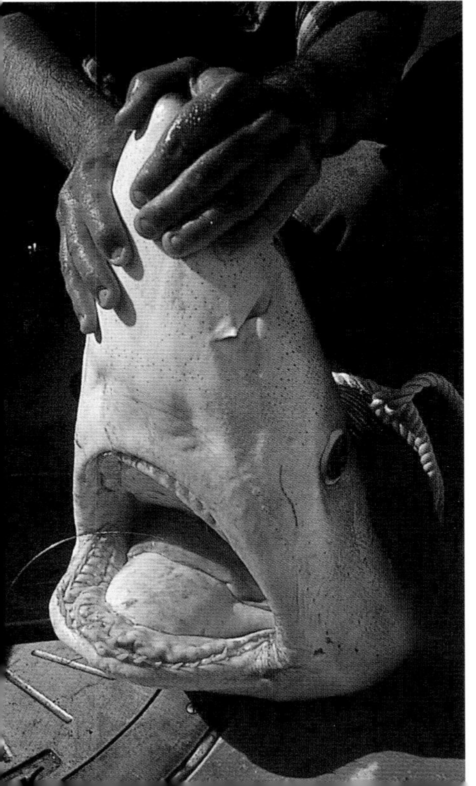

Above: Dusky sharks are sometimes spotted over the *Andrea Doria*. Below left: Is this blue shark enamored by its reflection, or is it teasing the photographer? Below right: Tom proudly displays his catch of the day.

After all these exciting but frustrating dives, we were forced to give up our quest.

Spirits were at low ebb. The primary purpose of the trip had met with failure; anticipation gave way to depression. Reluctantly, we freed the grapnel and reset it in the stern of the wreck, where alternative plans were put into effect. Much of this massive ship remained to be explored, and many other artifacts were yet to be found, although no experience could match the grandeur of recovering the ship's bell.

In separate teams Mike and Kenny, and Bill and Artie, set out to search for a builder's plaque which photographs showed was mounted on an aft-facing bulkhead on the Sun Deck. They found that the thin metal superstructure had long since rusted away. During the course of their dive, Mike and Kenny ducked into a room and found several pieces of china and glassware, emblazoned or etched with the "Italia" crest and crown.

Tom and I elected to check out the stern steering station, where the auxiliary helm and navigating equipment should still be in place. I had been on several cruise ships in the past, and knew what could be found there.

The afternoon sun was high when we made our dive, and visibility on the wreck was a clear thirty feet. From where the anchor line was placed we had to swim 175 feet along the hull, at a depth of 170 feet, to reach our goal. We kicked hard, but did not dare to get out of breath. We avoided streamers of monofilament and clots of netting that wrapped the wreck like a package.

Courtesy of the Italian Line.

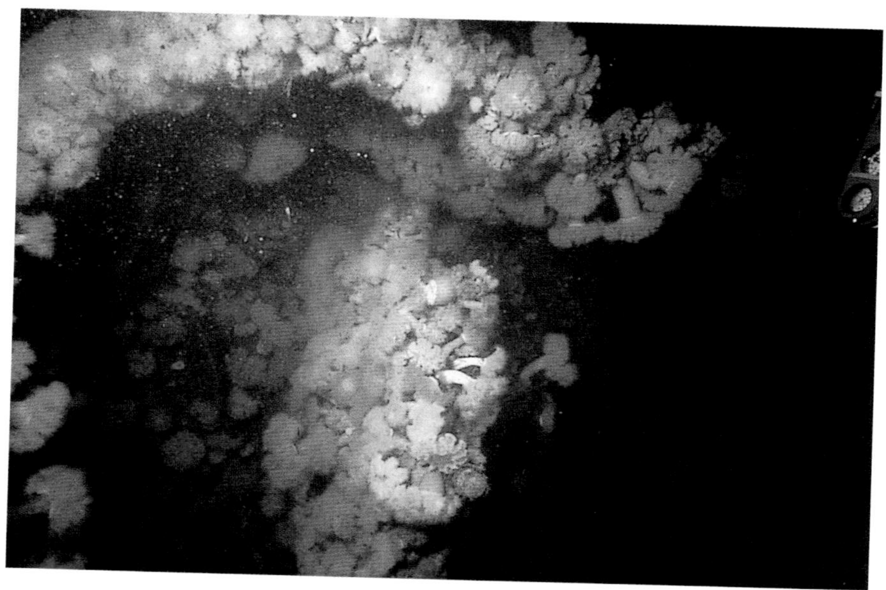

When the stern bridge wing loomed up, we checked gauges and exchanged okay signs. Letting air out of my suit, I dropped down the rear bulkhead of the back deck. I shone my light down past my flippers. No current moved the graceful anemones feeding with their delicate tentacles on floating microplankton. I kept one eye on my depth gauge.

At 200 feet the visibility was still good. Below me was a curved railing so festooned with feeding anemones that I could barely make out the individual cross pipes. The railing circled a spoked shape that could be nothing other than a wooden steering wheel. It was four feet across.

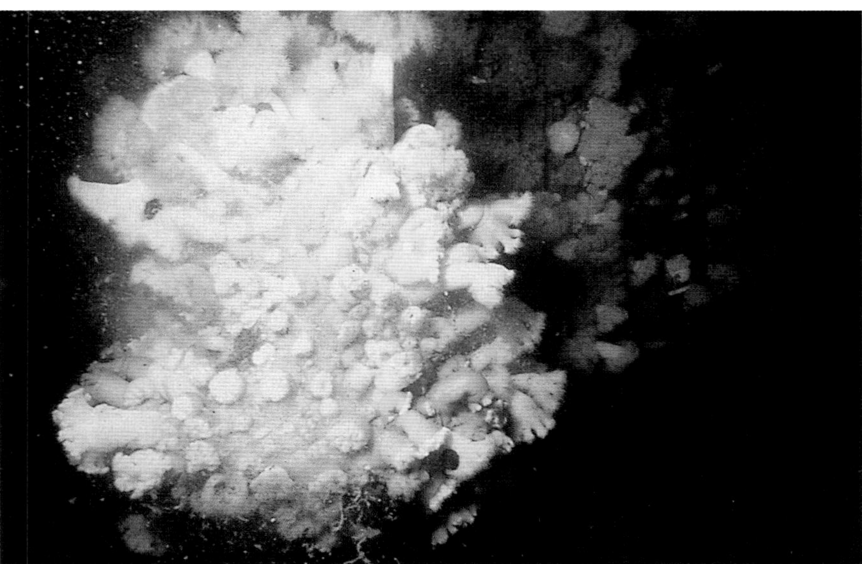

I brought my camera to bear, and aligned the strobe. The brilliant flash of light was momentary, but it was enough to capture the helm on film. I bracketed for exposure by getting closer, shooting again. I put my foot on the lower rail in order to steady myself as I adjusted my buoyancy and scanned the area with my light.

Then I saw it, hanging on a thick steel shaft attached to the after bulkhead. Eight inch long anemones crowded every square inch of surface, their tentacles waving fanlike. Except for the vague outline, it was a near perfect disguise. I held my camera to my mask, depressed the shutter release as I swam closer. I reached out and touched it. It did not move.

I stuck my hand up inside, but the clapper was gone. I backed away. I steadied myself on the rail again, cocked the shutter, and fired again. A shadow dropped down in front of me, and I heard a loud whooping. Tom was in front of me; he, too, had seen the bell and recognized it for what it was.

Those other cruise ships, too, had had stern bells. That was what compelled me to inspect this section of the wreck, hoping that the *Andrea Doria* was no different.

Tom's eyes were radiant. He continued to whoop through his regulator, and I could make out the words "All right!" in a high-pitched screech. He was not shy about showing emotion. He shook my hand, grabbed my shoulder, pulled me close and hugged me.

And to think that we had almost given up.

There was important work to be done, so I set about doing it. Letting my camera rig dangle from my wrist by the lanyard, I took out my knife and started scraping the anemones from their home. First I cleaned off the stanchion to see how the bell was attached. A thick bolt with a large hexagonal nut held it firmly in place. Then, as Tom held the light for me, I ran the stainless steel blade down the side of the bell. Bronze glinted through the nicked encrustation, and the bell shape began to appear. I was not even aware of the anemones plummeting into the darkness; they would have to find a new home.

At first, the bell appeared to be blank, with no name. I was sorely disappointed. Even if we recovered the bell, no one would believe that it came from the wreck of the *Andrea Doria*. It was not until I had scraped clean more than half its surface that the word "Andrea" appeared. Some of the red paint still filled in the grooves. The arched lettering spelled out "Andrea Doira," and underneath was the date of manufacture, "1952."

I backed away, motioning Tom to pose next to the bell. I snapped a series of photographs. Then, since we had only five minutes remaining in our dive, and a long swim ahead of us, we reluctantly left it behind. During the hour long decompression we smiled at each other, shook hands, and rocked hysterically. But we were unable to talk; it was frustrating to say the least. It was with great relief that I clambored up the ladder to our waiting companions and related triumphantly what we had found.

Our fourth day over the wreck was one of jubilation. A bolt of vitality had been injected into all of us. At last, our dreams coalesced into tangibility. We hastily devised a plan to slip a mesh bag around the bell, attach a liftbag, partially inflate it, and knock out the bolt. That way, when the bell fell off the stanchion it would not drop to the sand, but would float free. If all went well, we could be on our way home that night.

Above: Tom poses with the bell.

Right: John, Tom, and Bill take up basket weaving.

All did not go well. Breaking our tradition of making only one dive a day, Mike and Kenny drew the unglamorous task of moving the anchor line closer to the stern. Then Bill and Artie made a second dive as the sun settled low in the western sky. They removed the nut, but did not drive out the bolt. Much to their chagrin, they discovered that I had underestimated the diameter of the bell; with all their strength they were unable to stretch the nylon mesh around its base.

Nor did we have on board a bag large for our needs. We had to make our own. John cut three hundred feet of polypropylene rope into fifteen foot lengths. Tom burned the ends to prevent unravaling. We cleared the after deck and laid out the pieces. Then John and Bill wove a gigantic basket. The job took hours. But at this point there was no sense in doing it half right.

That night the sea kicked up. We devised a plan so that each team had a specific task to perform. I slept restlessly. Early in the morning, Tom and I suited up for the first dive. The short chop was making me sick, so I told Tom I was not feeling well. I moved sluggishly, and suffered a mild headache. To make matters worse, when I put my regulators on my tanks, the high pressure hose burst. Without it I could not tell how much air I had during the dive.

Kenny had a spare, but this posed a problem. All my other gauges were on a console bolted to the tank pressure gauge; it would take quite a while to disassemble them all in order to insert the new gauge. As an expedient, I simply used plastic tie-wraps to lash my gauge panel onto Kenny's pressure gauge. Tom and I got into the water without delay.

At 210 feet we used the spokes of the auxiliary steering helm as hangers for our mesh equipment bags. When Tom pulled out the giant, handmade basket, it kept coming like a magician's neverending handkerchief. The polypropylene hovered around us like a movie monster spider's web. We pulled the unwieldy contraption around the bell. When it was secured, I held it in place while he put enough air into the 500-pound liftbag (already attached) to keep the basket from slipping off. It took most of our allotted twenty minutes.

When the job was completed, and while Tom was checking to make sure the basket fitted properly, I perfunctorily glanced at my air gauge.

It read zero.

I reacted like any other experienced diver: I panicked, and took immediate safety steps. With one hand I grabbed for the spare regulator hanging around my neck. The pony bottle contained an extra twenty cubic feet of air. With my other hand I grabbed Tom by the arm, shook him violently, and waved the gauge panel in front of him.

He promptly stopped what he was doing. He was prepared to act as soon as I communicated to him my problem. At the same time, and in a flash of insight, I realized that I had read the wrong gauge: the one with the burst hose that held my other gauges. Tom watched wonderingly as I spun the gauge panel around and read Kenny's replacement. I had used only half my air, and had plenty in reserve. Feeling foolish, I gave him the okay sign. He nodded with a shrug. I could not tell him about my stupid mistake until we surfaced.

During the hour long decompression the queasy feeling in my stomach grew worse. The sea state was increasing; the bouncing motion of the boat against the waves jerked the anchor line unmercifully. The dull throb in my head became agonizing stabs of pain behind my eyes. Desparately, I fought to quell the nausea.

I was never so happy for a decompression stage to end. I climbed weakly up the aluminum ladder onto the pitching deck of the *Seeker*. Tom reported our progress while I sat dully, too sick to get undressed. It was not until after Mike and Kenny hit the water that I summoned the energy to get out of my suit. Sill in my long underwear, I limped below and crashed into a bunk. The boat bobbed like a cork; I felt as agitated as a sneaker in a washing machine.

Meanwhile, underwater, Mike and Kenny worked together like a well oiled machine. As Mike inflated the liftbag from a spare bottle, Kenny attached a safety line to the basket and unreeled it as he ascended to the shallow part of the hull at 170 feet: not an easy task considering that it took both hands to manage the reel while he kicked upward, without being able to handle his buoyancy control valves. He lodged the reel in a crevice. Mike finished filling the liftbag. Their job was complete.

Now came the final moment, the one for which Bill had been waiting for all these years. We had left for him the all important task of driving out the pin and actually sending up the bell. He and Artie splashed down with their tools, and dropped straight down to the support stanchion. With Artie holding the light, Bill started pounding against the thick bolt with a three-pound hammer and a heavy-duty drift pin punch. The steel bolt was rusted in place, and moved only fractions of an inch with each hit. Bill pounded without stopping for a solid ten minutes before the pin backed beyond the first steel ear. Then the 150 pound bell cocked, wedging the pin with its weight. Artie had to work the bell back up into position where the pin was aligned, so Bill could continue driving it out. Only someone as strong as Artie could hang onto the stanchion with one hand and maneuver the bell with the other.

The bolt moved imperceptibly. Bill's arm was giving out from swinging the heavy hammer. He paused after every few swings in order to rest tired muscles. He was breathing hard, and the pain in his biceps was agonizing. Still he swung—and swung.

Artie watched the end of the bolt protrude more and more with each pounding crash of iron on iron. When he thought it was ready to come out, he swam to the upper hull, picked up the safety reel, and locked his legs around a beam. He peered over the edge of the deck, shining his light down at the inflated liftbag, and waited for the ascent.

The pin jumped out, the bell fell into the basket, the contraption soared off for the surface—and a loop of polypropylene snagged on the projecting bell stanchion.

With nearly 500 pounds of lift in the bag, Bill was unable to pull the basket back down to untangle it. Underwater, buoyancy exerts the same force as dead weight on land. Bill pulled the liftbag release cord to let out some air. He also checked his gauges, and realized that it was time to terminate the dive. At that depth one does not overextend oneself. Air is consumed too fast, decompression penalties climb too rapidly, time is too short in case of emergency. Reluctantly, he was forced to leave. The bell was left hanging literally by a thread.

All during Bill's and Artie's exertions, I had my face buried under the pillows: the barest glimmer of light caused intense pain in my eyes. My forehead was hot with fever. This was no simple case of seasickness, but the beginning bouts of the flu. Lying on a rocky boat in six foot seas did not mitigate my condition at all.

After five days at sea in a small boat with only four bunks, we were all feeling cramped. The constant climbing over gear was exhausting. We were low on drinking water; our ice had melted, so we had no cold drinks and our food was going bad: some had to be ditched. If the bell did not come up immediately, we would have to pull anchor and head for shore for provisions.

The compressor was started up for the last time; the tanks were refilled. Even though everyone had already made his dive for the day, it was decided to make one last effort to recover the bell. The repetitive dive would require extended decompression, so as much surface interval as possible was worked into the schedule.

The afternoon dragged. I lolled in a half stupor, lying in the communal bunk in a mass of damp sleeping bags, with my arms wrapped around a plastic bucket—in case I could not make it to the head in time for an unpleasant experience. I had very little awareness of what was going on.

Finally, late in the day, after waiting as long as they could, Tom, Mike, and Kenny, prepared their gear. Tom asked me to explain my procedures for extrapolating decompression requirements from the Navy Tables. The Tables were inadequate for this dive because they offered no repetitive group letter for a dive deeper than 190 feet. What I had done in the past was to extend the graph on which the printed Tables were based, and calculated what that repetitive group letter should have been for the specific depth. Now, of course, I relied upon a decompression computer with its own built in formula, but I was the only one on the boat using one. Sitting in the dark, wearing a pair of sunglasses, I drew out a dive profile so Tom could figure his decompression stops. I did the same for Mike and Kenny.

Tom, Mike, and Kenny dove as a team, with individual tasks strictly defined. With clocklike precision they went about their jobs as they had rehearsed them. Kenny cleared the safety line and reattached the reel. Mike deflated the liftbag just enough to let the weight of the bell drag it down. Tom pulled the basket free of the projection. Mike reinflated the liftbag from the attached tank. Then things got a little out of control.

The whole assembly started sinking toward the bottom before Mike could get enough air in it. Tom stuck his mouthpiece under the bag and pushed the purge, adding air from his own tanks. Still the bag and bell sank—to be saved by the grace of a poor fisherman who had lost his diamond jig while fishing for cod. The basket snagged on a solitary strand of monofilament—again hanging by a thread—allowing Mike and Tom the time to add more air to the liftbag.

Slowly, the bell moved upward. Tom kept the basket clear as it passed the crucial stanchion. Mike got out of the way so he would not become entangled as the basket passed by. Kenny held onto the safety reel as the bell passed him, gathering speed. The line whipped off the reel with rapid acceleration. The liftbag ballooned to full capacity and burst clear out of the water. When it settled back down, the bell dropped the length of the connecting rope, pulling the bottom of the bag underwater before the air could escape. It rose and fell in the waves.

Kenny tied the safety line to the wreck. This way, should the bag sink before it could be hoisted aboard the boat, a diver could return to where the line was tied in, and follow it out to the sand where the bell would be sitting at the end of it. The safety line also prevented the liftbag from drifting away in the current.

John holds onto the safety line while Artie (in the water) double checks the knot. Bill waits to grab the liftbag as it swings alongside the boat.

Aboard the *Seeker*, Artie was already in his suit. Without tanks, he leaped into the spuming, wind-swept sea and swam an additional safety line from the boat. He was taking no chances. Once he attached the nylon rope to the basket, he cut the bottom safety line. He and the bell drifted toward the thirty-five foot fiberglas cork.

From down below I heard the commotion and the shouts of glee. I struggled out of the bunk, shielding my eyes, and grabbed my camera. I spotted the liftbag in the churning ocean. I promptly leaned over the rail and puked.

With a broad grin on his face, John shouted up to Bill, on the bridge, "Gary's so excited he threw up."

I cleaned out my mouth with fresh water and started taking pictures. Artie ducked under the surface and attached the winch line. Bill and John started hauling on the pulley. When the basket came out of the water, instead of repositioning the winch line lower, Bill and John, full of exuberance, leaned over the gunwale, grabbed the polypropylene, and manhandled the basket over the side.

The bell was on deck. Mission accomplished.

It was another seventy minutes before the three-man dive team finished decompressing. As soon as they climbed aboard, John started the engine and Artie cut the anchor line. We were on the way home.

Later, while Bill broke out the champagne, Artie pulled out our file of *Andrea Doria* deck plans and photographs. He studied them meticulously. "Look at this picture of the *Doria* sinking. Do you see a bell in it?"

Several shots of the *Andrea Doria* clearly, showed the forward bell hanging from its peculiarly shaped tripod davit. But the post-collision Coast Guard photo to which he was referring, taken from an airplane as the liner was listing sharply, seemed different. After careful consideration, and study with a magnifying glass, I had to admit that on the sinking photo there was no bell, only an empty davit. Then Bill pointed out that what we had mistook for the bell davit on the bow was in fact the loading boom for number one hold. Underwater, covered with marine growth and anemones, it had been impossible to tell.

Courtesy of the U.S. Coast Guard.

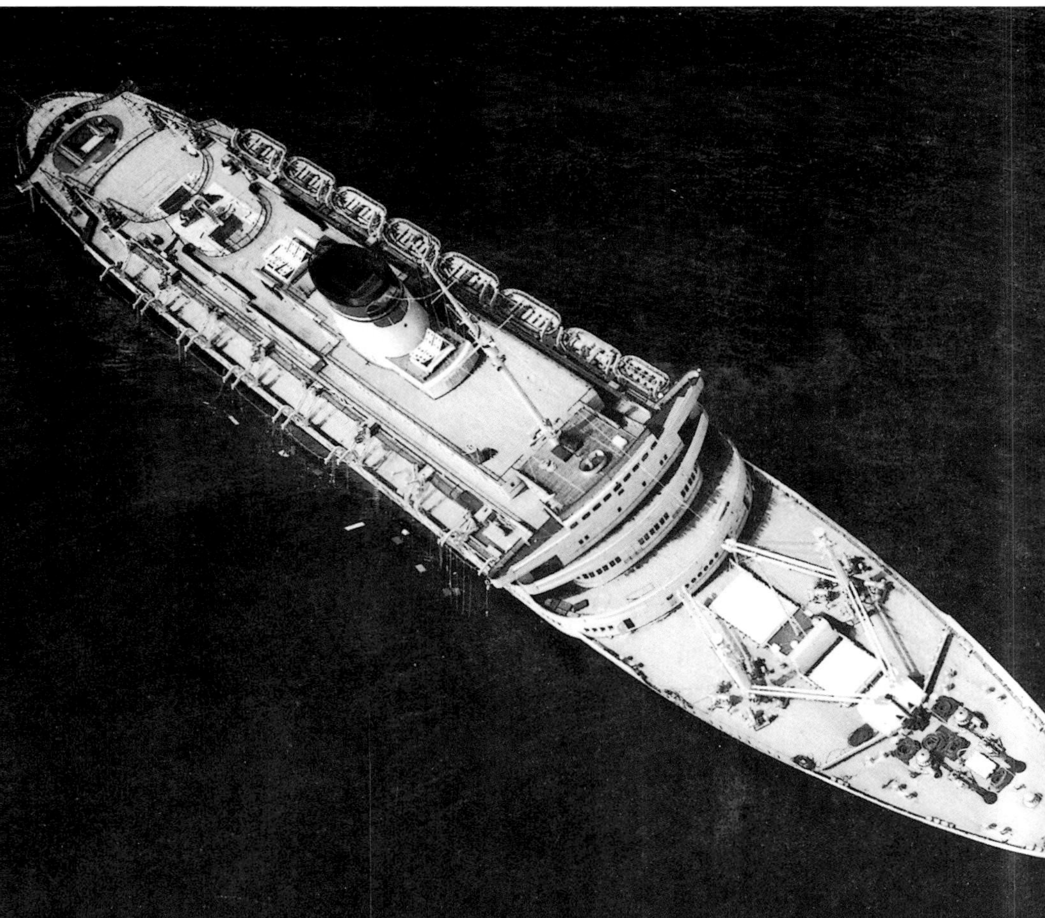

Long before the *Andrea Doria* took her nose dive to the bottom of the cold Atlantic, her bow bell was missing. Had it been removed prior to her last trip? Had it been repositioned in the stern? Had it been knocked off its mount by the force of the collision? Had it been removed by crew members before the sinking? It was a mystery, and to this day it remains a mystery.

It is possible that Edward Rowe Snow, ship historian and prolific writer of sea tales, could have solved the mystery. In the January 1966 issue of *Yankee*, he wrote, "In the garage of my home at Marshfield, Massachussetts is a large bell marked *Andrea Doria 1953*. The story of how I acquired this bell is still classified material, and cannot be told for several years." When Snow passed away in 1976, he took his secret with him. His widow still resides at the same address, still has possession of the bell; but she does not admit to knowing how her husband acquired it. Some day, perhaps, the secret will unfold. Hopefully, it will tie in with the missing bell and davit depicted by the Coast Guard photos. I am only one among many who continue to wonder.

The bell in Snow's back yard is brazed all the way around, as if it had been broken in two and repaired: another mystery. Photo by John Moyer.

The seven happy divers are (standing, left to right) the author, Art Kirchner, Mike Boring, Tom Packer (high), Kenny Gascon (low), and (sitting, left to right) Bill Nagle, John Moyer.

With *our* bell hoisted up on the winch boom, Artie made the official incantation. "This is the bell from the *Andrea Doria*, sunk on July 26, 1956, and rung now for the first time in twenty-nine years."

He tapped the inside with a rusty hammer and, despite the coating of marine growth, a sound that was as clear and melodic as—well, as a bell—tolled the achievement of our deed. It was the sweet tintinabulation of success.

Still a hundred miles from Montauk, with the divers not even out of their soggy long johns, the radio crackled with an urgent message from the Coast Guard. John descended the ladder from the flying bridge and cornered Tom in the crowded cabin. "It's a girl."

For a moment, Tom was as speechless as he was expressionless. When the impact of the statement became clear to him, he burst into a grinning jumping jack, shouting and shaking hands. It was a momentous day in his life. We all shared his jubilation.

Kim was safe, the baby was healthy; but she refused to name her Andrea.

From her magnificent beginning to her ignominous end, the Grand Dame of the Sea captured the imagination of an era. Above: Passing El Morro, San Juan, Puerto Rico. Courtesy of The Steamship Historical Society of America. Below: Courtesy of the U.S. Coast Guard.

AFTERWORD

"You can be told about a thing a hundred times. It is better to see it just once."

—Ho Chi Minh

Above left: Jon Hulburt recovered the barnacle encrusted flower pot from the Winter Garden. Above right: Steve Gatto recovered the stern steering helm. Below: The *Wahoo* reflects a somber mood.

Afterword

The *Andrea Doria's* bell has attracted a great deal of attention, so it has done a fair amount of traveling: for display, for symposiums, for slide presentations. Prior to one such occasion, after Bill Nagle had placed the bell in the back of his pickup truck, his wife Ashley went to visit a friend. She drove the truck through the countryside on narrow, backwoods lanes. When she got to her friend's house, Ashley thought she would show off the bell. Imagine her shock and horror when she discovered the tailgate down and the bell gone. It had rolled out somewhere along the circuitous route between townships.

Ashley immediately called the police, and explained her predicament. Rather than laughing her off as another kook, the officer told her that a lady had just called saying she had *found* a big bronze bell lying in the middle of the road. It was too heavy for her to lift, but since she lived nearby she went home and got her father to help her pick it up and load it into the trunk of her car. She was an honest person, and wanted only to return the item to the rightful owner.

With sincere praise and undisguised relief (Bill was understandably upset) Ashley recovered the one-hundred-fifty pound bell. It suffered one gash and a few nicks, but was otherwise none the worse for wear. However, it was suggested that for her carelessness she should be awarded the "No bell" prize.

The odyssey of the *Andrea Doria* continues. Aside from the chimerical *Ark*, she is one of the greatest treasure ships in history. She offers her neverending riches to all those who visit her. Her real wealth is valued not in dollars and cents, or in lire, but in the seductive experience she offers to all those who pay tribute to her remains.

One such tribute was paid by Bill Campbell, whose fascination for diving, for the *Andrea Doria*, and for all things nautical, culminated in the design and production of a twenty-five year commemorative plaque which he, Steve Bielenda, and Hank Keatts placed on the liner's encrusted hull.

Further praise is expressed by Dave Bright, whose personal collection of *Andrea Doria* memorabilia exceeds all others, and which includes a lifeboat which for years had been lying forgotten in the weeds adjacent to a Staten Island power plant. His hope for establishing a permanent museum exhibit is nearly a reality.

Top and middle: Steve Gatto took these shots of the warning sign a year apart. (See the photo on page 160, and look under the stern wing.) One can see how the nets shifted. Bottom: Bill Nagle and the sign after its recovery.

Sadly, the wreck of the *Andrea Doria* continues to deteriorate. Fifteen to twenty feet of her starboard hull has sunk into the sand, drawn irresistibly ever deeper by the forces of Nature. Her superstructure is sloughing off like bark peeling off a rotten tree. During one of my sixty-six dives to the wreck, I entered the First Class Ball Room only to find myself looking outside through a web of trawler nets. Where the ceiling of the Ball Room should have been there gaped a fifty-foot hole: everything above was gone, from the Boat Deck to the Bridge.

As the structural integrity of the wreck is compromised by corrosion and unnatural stress, the lower decks will be the next to collapse. Soon, the *Andrea Doria* will be nothing but a massive, empty hulk, like a scooped out half-watermelon. A huge pile of debris will fan across the sand, subject to the errant, quickly changing tides and to swift currents that will either bury or sweep away any recognizable relics left uncrushed. As an historic resource she is being whittled away. There is no preservation in the open sea.

Today, however, she is yet a silent testimonial to an era long past. Her condition is one which should encourage aficionados to capture her glamor while it lasts.

Just as Peter Gimbel opened the way to the great white shark, he opened the way to the *Andrea Doria*. The way remains open. A never ending treadmill of admirers make annual pilgramages to the *Andrea Doria's* final resting place. They are a special breed of people: they go unheralded, unsung, but are ever present. They number only in the scores, and, grasping with relish the challenge of the deep, they seek nothing more than the thrill of excitement and the quest of adventure.

A steady stream of charter boats plies a well worn path to that historic spot south of Nantucket, carrying divers of experience who crave for stimulation in an otherwise calm and peaceful world. Some want to photograph this underwater monument. Some wish to acquire a souvenir of their achievement. But most just want to be able to say—I have touched her.

Whatever the reason, the *Andrea Doria* will continue to attract attention in the world of diving. She will always be there, like the unassailable mountain to the climber. In the minds and the hearts of many she will never be forgotten.

The *Andrea Doria* still lives.

Bibliography

Films

Armstrong Circle Theater (1956) *S.O.S. from the Andrea Doria* (a dramatization aired October 16 on channel 4, New York).
CBS (1966) *Day of Disaster* (Aired March 24).
Gimbel, Peter (1975) *The Mystery of the Andrea Doria* (Aired March 24, 1976).
——— (1981) *Andrea Doria: the Final Chapter* (Aired August 16, 1984).
Vailati, Bruno (1968) *Fate of the Andrea Doria.*

Books

Carletti, Stephano (1968) *Andrea Doria* (published in Italy).
Hoffer, William (1979) *Saved!*, Summit Books, New York.
Mattson, Algot (1980) *The House of Brostrom: Portrait of a World Company*, Askild & Karnekull, Stockholm, Sweden.
McKenney, Jack (1983) *Dive to Adventure*, Panorama Publications Ltd., Vancouver, Canada (Compilation of the author's articles listed separately below).
Monasterio, Aurelio (1957) *Tragedy on the Andrea Doria* (published in Mexico by B. Costa-Amic).
Moscow, Alvin (1959) *Collision Course*, G.P. Putnam's Sons, New York, reprinted 1981 by Grosset & Dunlap, New York.
Titanic Commutator (1981) Summer, Volume 5, Number 1, Titanic Historical Society (Special twenty-fifth anniversary issue).

Articles

American Red Cross (1956) "Ships in the Night: Red Cross Relief Operations Following Collision of Andrea Doria—Stockholm," Report of the New York Chapter of the American Red Cross, July 25.
Baekeland, G. Brooks, and Peter Gimbel (1964) "By Parachute into Peru's Lost World," *National Geographic Magazine*, August.
Carrothers, John C. (1957) "Uneasy Lies the Head that Wears a Crown," U.S. Naval Institute *Proceedings*, January.
——— (1958) "There Must Have Been a Third Ship!" U.S. Naval Institute *Proceedings*, July.
——— (1972) "The Andrea Doria—Stockholm Disaster: Was There a Conspiracy?" *Safety At Sea International*, December.
——— (1986) "Andrea Doria: Thirty Years Later, the Contraversy Continues," *Titanic Commutator*, Volume 10, Number 3, Titanic Historical Society.
Castillo, Angel (1981) "A New Debate Arises on Why Andrea Doria Was Lost in '56 Crash," *New York Times*, October 26.
Centa, Elinor T. (1973) "The Doria Entertains a Lady," *Skin Diver*, April.
Cole, William D., (1958) "Treasure Below!" *Argosy*, August.
de Camp, Michael A. (1967) "Unreal Trip to the Andrea Doria," *Skin Diver*, January.
Dickenson, Fred (1967) "The Tantalizing Treasure of the Andrea Doria," *True*, November.
Dugan, James (1974) "Andrea Doria," *Skin Diver*, August.
Giddings, Al (1969) "The Andrea Doria: Everest of the Sea," *Skin Diver*, January.
Gimbel, Peter (1956) "Camera in a Sea Tomb," *Life*, August 13.
Gimbel, Peter (1957) "Down to 'Doria' Again," *Life*, October 28.

Lord, Walter (1956) "An Epic Sea Rescue," *Life*, August 6.

MacLeish, Kenneth (1956) "Divers Explore the Sunken 'Doria'," *Life*, September 17.

Maddocks, Melvin (1978) "A Litany of Disasters on the Devil Sea," from *The Great Liners*, Time-Life Books.

Marine Engineer and Naval Architect (1953) "Machinery of the 'Andrea Doria'," January and February.

Matteson, Leonard J. (1956) "The 'Andrea Doria' Disaster—A Composite of the Marine Insurance Problem," *Weekly Underwriter*, December 8 and December 15.

McKenney, Jack (1970) "The Great Underwater Wreck Robbery," *Skin Diver*, January.

——— (1974) "Andrea Doria Caper," *Skin Diver*, January and February.

——— (1976) "The Mystery of the Andrea Doria," *Skin Diver*, March.

——— (1982) "Andrea Doria Treasure," *Skin Diver*, March and April.

Metcalfe, Jack (1968) "Adventure at 40 Fathoms," Sunday News, August 11.

Mielke, Otto (1959) "Rammed, Capsized, and Sunk," Chapter 2 in *Disaster at Sea*," Souvenir Press, London.

Miley, Donald F. (1960) "Who Is in Command?" U.S. Institute *Proceedings* October.

National Underwriter (1956) August 2, 16, September 6.

Newsweek (1956) "As a Ship Lay Dying in the Night," August 6.

Newsweek (1957) "To Make a Ship Live," August 12.

Norris, Martin J. (1960) "Why They Can't Raise the Andrea Doria," *Saga*, October.

Oliver, Edward F. (1957) "The Sea Rescue of the Century," *Ships and the Sea*, Winter.

Parks, Ramsey (1957) "Exploration of the Sunken Liner Andrea Doria," *Skin Diver*, June.

Pinto, Allen (1981) "Historic Lifeboat Found in Arthur Kill's Back Yard," *Around the System*, September.

Ronberg, Gary (1982) "Raiders of the Lost Liner," *Today*, Philadelphia *Inquirer* Magazine, September.

Ryan, Cornelius (1956) "Five Desparate Hours in Cabin 56," *Colliers*, September.

Sherwood, John E. (1958) "How We'll Raise the Andrea Doria," *Popular Mechanics*, August.

——— (1959) "Contents of Andrea Doria Strong Room to Be Raised!" *Skin Diver*, April.

Shipbuilding and Shipping Record (1953) "The 'Andrea Doria' and the 'Cristoforo Colombo'," August 13.

Snow, Edward Rowe (1963) "All But 45 Were Saved," *Yankee*, August.

Sparks, Fred (1957) "He Dives to the 'Doria'," *U.S. Coast Guard Magazine*, June.

Time (1956) "Disasters: Against the Sea," August 6.

Town & Country (1982) "Rapture of the Deep," June.

Tzimoulis, Paul J. (1964) "The Return of Andrea Doria," *Skin Diver*, December.

United States House of Representatives, 34th Congress, 2d Session (1957) "Safety of Life at Sea Study," January 3.

Weekly Underwriter (1956) July 28, August 4, 11, 18, 25, September 1, 8, 15, 22, October 13, December 8; (1957) January 5, 12, 19, 26, February 2, 16, 23, April 6, May 11, 18, July 13, August 3, 10, September 7, November 17.

Wood, Alden S. (1957) "Andrea Doria Entombed," *Water World*, March-April.

Young, Robert T. (1981) "Collision in the Night: The End of the *Andrea Doria*," *USA Today*, July.

Courtesy of the Italian Line.

Books by Gary Gentile

Nonfiction

Diving

Advanced Wreck Diving Guide
Andrea Doria: Dive to an Era
Wreck Diving Adventures

Nautical History

Track of the Gray Wolf
USS San Diego: the Last Armored Cruiser
Popular Dive Guide Series:
Shipwrecks of Delmarva
Shipwrecks of New Jersey

Fiction

Underwater Adventure

The Peking Papers

Science Fiction

Return to Mars
Silent Autumn
The Time Dragons Trilogy:
A Time for Dragons
Dragons Past
No Future for Dragons

Supernatural

The Lurker

Vietnam

Lonely Conflict

"The *Andrea Doria* strikes you as the very soul of desolation. The over-all impression of that wreck is one of enormity. It is as if you are seeing a vision. . . . there is almost life there."

—Peter Gimbel

Courtesy of The Steamship Historical Society of America.